IT'S INEVITABLE:
Customized Teaching and Learning

A Fieldbook For and From the Field

James D. Parry, Ph.D.
Nancy Hall, Ed.D.
Patricia Peel, Ed.D.

ISBN: 1477605495
ISBN-13: 9781477605493

Table of Contents

It's Inevitable: Customized Teaching and Learning

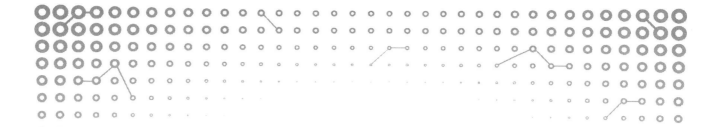

Acknowledgements

Synergy. That sums it up.

It started when a long-time colleague, Chuck Schwahn, stopped by my office to share his most recent work on a book titled *inevitable*. Co-authored with Bea McGarvey, *inevitable* puts forward a powerful vision for schools. Branded as Mass Customized Learning (MCL), the vision emphasizes a learner-centered approach and capitalizes on the potential of Information Age technologies. Chuck and Bea's vision is surpassed only by their passion to transform schools for the needs of learners in the 21st Century. Truly, *inevitable* captures the attention of readers because it makes so much sense. It spurs us to let go of "schools as we know them" and embrace "schools as they could be and should be!"

Chuck invited me to get on board as a partner with the vision of MCL. That didn't take much persuading. As the former director and ongoing champion of a non-profit professional development organization focused on innovation in education, the MCL vision was energizing! I felt compelled to join Chuck and Bea on this journey because I believe it is the most urgent challenge and opportunity for schools in recent decades. It confronts the limitations and fallacies of traditional schools and directs our attention toward "what should be" rather than "what has been."

As the momentum around the vision built, so did *inevitable* readers' questions about where and how to get started with MCL. Believers sought direction about strategies for getting others on board as well as starting points for implementing the vision. Soon Chuck and Bea recognized the need and potential of a how-to manual, or *fieldbook*, to support stakeholders with next steps in their journey to implement the MCL vision. At their invitation, I took on the role of spearingheading that work and served as editor for the *fieldbook* you are now reading.

The non-profit, professional development organization I referred to earlier is Technology and Innovation in Education (TIE), a branch of Black Hills Special Services Cooperative. Julie Mathiesen, my successor as director, and other TIE leaders keep me involved as a partner. As a result, the *fieldbook* is a collaborative venture that reflects the commitment and support of TIE leaders and colleagues. The *fieldbook* became a reality because TIE leaders perceive the value of this work and embrace the opportunity to be advocates and champions of the vision of customized teaching and learning. They embrace Chuck and

Bea as collaborators. They support me in my role as editor of the *fieldbook*. And, TIE will continue to be a premier leader and resource for implementing the vision in the years ahead.

While the *fieldbook* represents the interest and investment of many worthy contributors, the core of the work was shaped by a small executive team. Team member Nancy Hall, an experienced author, is former Dean of Education for Black Hills State University. And team member Pat Peel, an experienced practitioner, is the former Assistant Superintendent for the Douglas School District. Both Nancy and Pat possess a diversity of rich experience from the classroom to administrative roles. They continue their work in the education community as consultants. It was a privilege to serve as their team leader and benefit from their expertise and commitment to the *fieldbook* venture. Together, we realized so much about the potential of the vision of customized teaching and learning that our passion for the work grew as the *fieldbook* evolved.

Also, it is important to acknowledge the behind-the-scenes role of the West River Foundation. As a champion of this work and an advocate of education, the Foundation leadership endorsed the *fieldbook* at its inception and serves to forward the vision of customized teaching and learning in partnership with the authors and the other collaborating organizations.

So in a word, it is synergy. Essential elements and progressive forces combined in a timely manner to produce a tremendous opportunity with huge potential for impacting education. Chuck and Bea's compelling vision started that interaction. Appreciatively, that process involved and energized me and other colleagues along the way. We believe the resulting synergy is reflected in *It's inevitable: Customized Teaching and Learning*.

Gratefully,
James D. Parry, Ph.D.
Lead Editor

About the Authors and Editorial Team

James D. Parry, Ph.D., Lead Editor and Contributing Author

As founder and former director of Technology and Innovation in Education, Jim is respected for his forward thinking and progressive spirit with colleagues across the country. Organizational development is his forte. His expertise in systems is complemented by his practical insights stemming from his broad-based, firsthand experiences with leadership development, strategic planning, and technology integration across K-16. He understands the urgency for schools to pursue thoughtful, deliberate change in response to 21st Century realities. In his current education consultant role, he provides leadership and conducts presentations and workshops for innovative projects in education settings.

Nancy Hall, Ed.D., Editorial Team and Contributing Author

Nancy is a recognized innovator who has led system-wide changes in K-12 education and higher education. A cornerstone of her work is focusing organizational attention on a shared and inspirational vision, mission, core values and beliefs. She is passionate about building individual and collective capacity through professional development. Much of her work has been accomplished by developing synergy between educational and business organizations. She has co-authored three books including *Educating Oppositional and Defiant Children* by ASCD which won the Golden Lamp Award, the most prestigious award in the field of educational publishing. She is currently working as a writer and educational consultant.

Patricia Peel, Ed.D., Editorial Team and Contributing Author

If you've ever worked in the world where curriculum, instruction, assessment and staff development intersects with technology, you might have heard Pat say, "Tell me what I need to know about this technology so that I can best support your success." Being tutored by many fabulously talented and infinitely patient techies, she has had the privilege to facilitate teams of technology coordinators and, most recently, added technology department administrative oversight to her resume. The sum of these tech-related experiences has served as her customized learning plan and have left her with an un-dying gratitude for her too-many-to-count master tech-teachers. In recent days, her attention has turned to consultant and writing opportunities.

Charles Schwahn, Ph.D., Contributing Author

As the co-author of *inevitable*, Chuck reveals much about himself in his writing. He is candid about his humble roots and his launch into an education career. He is modest about his major accomplishments as a highly regarded educator and administrator, as a premier leadership developer and trainer, and as a distinguished co-author of respected writings such as ***Total Leaders***. But he is bold and articulate when it comes to sharing his vision for education in the 21ˢᵗ Century. His passion for Mass Customized Learning (MCL) reflects his genuine concern for learners and educators. Clearly, he is a champion of champions in America's education community.

Beatrice McGarvey, M.Ed., Contributing Author

Grounded in a rich tenure of classroom and administrative experience, Bea is—in a word—practical! She values research, current literature, and sage education leaders to inform her consultant work. Her knack for gleaning the nuggets and translating them into practical insights is extraordinary and highly valued. As the co-author of ***inevitable***, she is traveling the country instilling enthusiasm and energy for the potential of Mass Customized Learning (MCL). She challenges her education colleagues to embrace the power of technology and to invest in changing school structures for engaging learners meaningfully. Bea is a master at keeping the focus on the core issues and pursuing practical solutions which center on the needs of learners.

Julie Mathiesen, Ed.D., Contributing Author

As the current director of Technology and Innovation Education, Julie is recognized as both a regional and national thought leader in the arena of transformative technologies. Her presentations incorporate current and emerging examples of technology which make the vision of customized teaching and learning feasible and reachable. She energizes and encourages classroom practitioners and administrative leaders to leverage the engagement factor of technology tools as the key for transforming educational systems to meet the needs of 21st Century learners. As the chief learner at TIE, she embraces the potential of technology readily and models effective applications for her colleagues continually. Given her credibility, her voice is sought and respected in the national arena of education technology champions.

Maggie Austin, M.S., Contributing Author

Life changed when Maggie saw her first Macintosh computer. She immediately saw how this tool could transform learning and was part of the first generation of technology coordinators. After working with students K-16 integrating technology into all subject areas, her teaching shifted to working with teachers and principals. More recently, her work as a *Courage to Teach* facilitator is leading her to grapple with bigger questions about the effects of an increasing technology presence on our human spirit. She believes teaching and learning are enhanced by both strong relationships and the right tools.

Kris Baldwin, Ed.D., Contributing Author

Technology and teaching have both experienced immense change since Kris began teaching and learning with computers in the 90s. During this time, she has promoted effective uses of educational technology with instructors K-16, as a teacher, a staff development coordinator, a grant writer and program director, an educational technology consultant, and an instructional designer. Her research has focused on the implementation of technology as an innovation adoption process.

Sherry Crofut, M.S., Contributing Author

As a recipient of the Milken award and a National Board Certified educator, Sherry has demonstrated her expertise as a master classroom teacher. Now she is capitalizing on the opportunity to encourage and influence the practice of many educators in her role as a professional developer with TIE. Her heart still belongs to students so addressing the needs of today's learners through effective technology integration is her passion.

John Swanson, M.A., Contributing Author

John's expertise as a high-quality professional development provider is well known across the region. Drawing from his knowledge of research and his strong base of experience as a classroom teacher and school administrator, John provides sound, practical insights which empower education stakeholders. He believes schools need to challenge students to think for themselves so that they are as prepared as possible to be productive members of 21st Century society. His facilitation and presentation skills are described as engaging and practical and his workshops provide teachers with hands-on experience, intellectual stimulation, and a sense of humor.

Jo Hartmann: M.Ed.Ad., Grammarian

A long-time educator with a rich tenure of experience as an English/reading/composition teacher, administrator, and consultant, Jo is a prolific writer. As a former state teacher of the year, she is highly regarded by her colleagues as a model educator and champion of learners and learning. She currently authors two newsletters—more evidence of ongoing passion for writing. Born and raised in Great Britain, Jo has an eagle eye for grammar and an appreciation of her native tongue.

Megan Merscheim, Graphic Artist

An energetic, talented member of the Technology and Innovation in Education team, Megan produced the inviting design for the cover of the fieldbook.

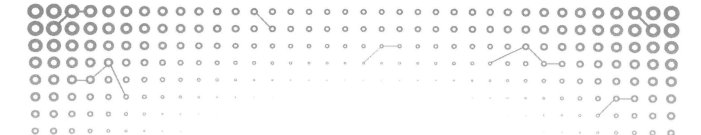

Introduction

The force driving our *fieldbook* development was a vision of sharing practical resources to support stakeholders with their implementation of a customized teaching and learning system for 21st Century schools. The executive editorial team recognized that the *fieldbook* should assist a diversity of stakeholders in a myriad of contexts. What might be a starting step for one school leader may not be the best opportunity for another. As a result, the *fieldbook* offers a plethora of resources for stakeholders, especially leaders.

Just as there are many onramps to the freeway, the *fieldbook* provides many entry points for stakeholders to ramp in to customized teaching and learning. Some stakeholders will ramp in by leading a book study of *inevitable* to grow a shared vision of MCL and gain the buy-in of key folks. Other stakeholders may ramp in by involving teams with an assessment of their status via the *Customized Teaching and Learning Rubric*. Yet other stakeholders may ramp in by engaging teachers with the resource titled *Teaching Differently* which captures the journey of a classroom teacher taking her first steps with implementation.

As the subtitle of "A Fieldbook For and From the Field" suggests, each resource has been crafted to include practical ideas and strategies for stakeholders in the trenches of schools. Equally important, those ideas and strategies are supported by experiences from the field as stakeholders embrace the vision of customized teaching and learning. As a result, the *fieldbook* resources are accompanied by stories where readers gain insights from other practitioners making progress with implementation.

Implementation of the customized teaching and learning vision is not a one-and-done proposition. The technology-based tools and systems to facilitate customization become more sophisticated every day. And the capabilities of digital curriculum products are more impressive all the time. Such reality requires that the *fieldbook* be a living resource for readers. Toward that end, links to current information, tools, and products will be noted at www.tie.net, the website for Technology and Innovation in Education. In this way, resources in the *fieldbook* will never be outdated.

Finally, it is important to note that the *fieldbook* is intended as a broad-based collection of possibilities rather than a comprehensive set of resources. Clearly, there are many viable ways to ramp in or enhance progress with implementation of the vision. As progress with implementation accelerates, there will be more and more ideas and strategies worthy of consideration by stakeholders. Thus, the *fieldbook* is positioned as a catalyst and contributor to the transformation our education system is experiencing in the 21st Century.

Getting Started with the *Fieldbook*

Each *fieldbook* resource includes, in this order:

- Resource Title
- Authors
- Connection to *inevitable* : The authors of each *fieldbook* resource note how the resource builds on a concept presented in *inevitable.* As a result, the resource enhances or operationalizes the concept in a practical and meaningful manner.
- Primary Topic: The primary topic (or topics) is noted for each *fieldbook* resource as a guide for the *fieldbook* user. The *fieldbook* is organized around four topic areas: Leadership, Teaching and Learning, Human Resources, and Technology Resources. These four areas align with the rubric presented in the first *fieldbook* resource titled *Facing Reality: An Audit.*
- Primary Audience
- Purpose
- Rationale
- Process for Use: As appropriate, authors of the resources provide basic descriptions of processes for implementing the resources productively and meaningfully.
- Story: Authors offer a personal experience or describe the experience of others to ground the *fieldbook* resource in real schools with real people facing the challenge of implementing customized teaching and learning.
- Going Forward: This section responds to the question of "what's next" with the concept addressed in the *fieldbook* resource. Writers make observations and offer insights from their perspectives about the future direction of implementation.
- References

At the front of the *fieldbook*, readers will discover a "Profile of Resources." It is a friendly and efficient tool for a quick overview of the substance of the *fieldbook*. The profile summarizes the "Primary Topic(s)" addressed by the resources so users may focus their implementation of the *fieldbook* as productively as possible.

The *Fieldbook*—The Time is Right

For the *fieldbook* authors, the *fieldbook* is about building momentum for a vision that is powerful and a change that is inevitable. Just a quick review of the resource titled: *Schools On the Move with Customization: Examples* confirms that a growing number of education stakeholders across the country are pursuing the vision—ramping in by investing in an opportunity that fits their context. For readers already invested in the vision of customized teaching and learning, the *fieldbook* offers affirmation as much as it empowers them with new ideas and strategies for next steps with implementation. For those considering a starting point, the *fieldbook* offers a friendly and comfortable entry to the implementation process. As a result, *fieldbook* users participate and contribute to the momentum associated with the MCL vision!

In the introduction of their book, Chuck and Bea share a quote attributed to Christopher Reeve: "At first dreams seem impossible, then improbable, and eventually . . . . inevitable." Chuck and Bea shared a dream for education. Their dream took form and became real as they described their vision for schools in the 21st Century. Clearly, their writing moved readers along on the journey noted by Reeve.

The authors of the *fieldbook* resources challenge education stakeholders to continue that journey by embracing the transformational vision and moving forward with implementation. The time is right. You have the opportunity to be part of the energy and excitement surrounding implementation. Start by exploring the *fieldbook* resources, collaborating with other stakeholders in your community, and identifying your next steps for reaching a vision that is—well, inevitable.

Acronyms—A Short List for Quick Reference

AP	Advanced Placement
ASCD	Association for Supervision and Curriculum Development
byod	bring your own device
IT	Instructional Technology
LMS	Learning Management System
MCL	Mass Customized Learning
NCLB	No Child Left Behind
NxGL	Next Generation Learning
OER	Open Education Resources
otb	out-of-the-box
PBL	Project Based Learning
PD	Professional Development
PLC	Professional Learning Community
R & D	Research and Development
SIS	Student Information System
TSI	Technology Support Index
WBWs	Weight Bearing Walls
1:1	One student for one technology device

Profile of Resources

Resource Title & Author(s)	Primary Topic			
	Leadership	Teaching and Learning	Human Resources	Technology Resources
Facing Reality: An Audit* (Hall)	X	X	X	X
A Book Study for Growing a Shared Vision* (Parry)	X	X	X	X
Schools on the Move with Customization: Examples (Swanson & Parry)	X	X	X	X
Weight Bearing Walls as Opportunities Rather than Barriers (Parry)	X	X		
On the Road to a Robust Technology System (Mathiesen)	X			X
Balancing Act: Theoretical and Practical (Peel)	X			X
Getting Ready for Rollout: Technology Assumption (Peel)	X			X
Minimizing the Risk; Maximizing the Decision* (Hall)	X		X	
Framework for Change (Peel)	X	X		
Recruiting and Hiring (Hall)	X		X	
Supervision for Alignment* (Hall and Schwahn)	X		X	
Rewarding and Recognizing Behaviors (Hall)			X	
Your Words Trigger What You Think (Schwahn & McGarvey)	X			
Learner Motivation: Do We Really Get It? (McGarvey)		X		
Teaching Differently: First Steps (Crofut & Peel)		X		X
Digital Content for Classrooms (Parry)		X		X
Developing a Mathematics Philosophy to Guide the Transition* (Austin)		X		
Exploring Online Mathematics Possibilities (Austin)		X		X
ePortfolios: Process and Assessment* (Peel)		X		X
Learning and Assessment in Real-Life Contexts* (Hall)		X		
Case Study: For the Field and from the Field (Peel)	X	X	X	X

*Tools accompany these resources

FACING REALITY: AN AUDIT

by Nancy Hall

⊙ Connection with *inevitable*

Chapter 1 of **inevitable** was written to motivate individuals to consider meaningful and transformational changes that will result in a customized delivery system for learning. The Facing Reality exercise builds upon Chapter 1 by describing an audit process and providing an audit tool. The audit tool enables your organization to evaluate where you are in relation to Mass Customized Learning (MCL). As Chuck and Bea articulated, "Once we begin to face these truths, without placing blame, we begin positioning ourselves, and our organization, to create meaningful and productive change."

⊙ Primary Topic

Leadership, Teaching and Learning, Human Resources, Technology Resources

⊙ Primary Audience

Key stakeholders are the primary audience for this exercise. Key stakeholders would include formal and informal leaders from among the following groups: teachers, learners, parents, administrators, and community members.

You are probably asking why not just involve formal leaders such as the PTA President, the School Board President, the Student Council President, Principals and the Superintendent, and the President of the Teachers' Association. These are important leaders to involve in this exercise, but in my experience there are other individuals who are just as critical to engage when beginning a system-change initiative. Think about who influences your school and your district (in positive and negative ways!). Who has respect and credibility among their peers? Who can think flexibly and creatively? Who has strong verbal communication skills and regularly uses these skills to persuade and influence others? Who is most energized by new ideas and demonstrates a strong work ethic? Who commits day in and day out to improving learner outcomes? As you think about these questions it becomes obvious that you need to include the "doers" in the change process. You will need to invite a critical mass of these individuals to join the formal leaders for this exercise.

Purpose

An initial audit can be used to motivate transformational change in your school/district. It can be used to affirm what customized learning concepts are firmly in place and to begin the dialogue and focus the energy of key stakeholders toward transformational growth. Have you ever attended a workshop that was so exciting and energizing that the discussion spilled over into the hallway during break? Have you been a part of a process in which participants kept talking about what was learned and reflecting upon new understandings for days after the group discussion concluded? That's the kind of outcome you are striving for!

An initial audit has the additional value in establishing a baseline to measure a district's growth toward customized learning over time. It is hard work for formal and informal leaders to make transformational change. We all need reinforcement. We need assurance and confirmation that our work is guiding us toward our preferred future for our learners. An audit can be repeated and reported on an annual basis to maintain momentum and guide the yearly focus.

Rationale

The rubric tool that has been developed for an audit of customized teaching and learning is new. We are working with early adopters to pilot its use. The key factors come directly from the *inevitable* vision and are described on pages 106 to 113 of the book.

Process for Use

I was fortunate to work with Chuck when he was an assistant superintendent in South Dakota and then again when he was doing consulting work relative to strategic planning in North Dakota. The process that I am going to describe for the audit is borrowed from one that I have seen Chuck use over and over with tremendous success in helping organizations prepare for transformational change. It is a process which will allow self-assessment through the lenses of various constituents, yielding an honest and transparent check on reality.

1. Establish diverse audit teams from the carefully selected group of key stakeholders. These teams will be working in a group setting to conduct an initial customized teaching and learning audit for your institution. For example, a team might be composed of one learner, one teacher leader, one administrator, and one community member with specialized knowledge of the school/district in a specific area of the rubric. Think about which personalities might work most effectively together to yield a lively professional discussion.

    I ask potential participants which area of the customized teaching and learning model interests them the most. I take painstaking efforts to build these work groups. I check my preliminary groupings with a few trusted colleagues to make sure I have a promising configuration. I don't place all the "Tommy Talkatives" together on one team or the "Nellie Naysayers" together. Instead of fostering motivation and energy toward transformational change, you could end up fostering frustration, irritation, or worse yet.....resistance to change!

2. As you prepare to invite the key stakeholders to be a part of an audit team session, get your creative juices flowing and be your best inspirational self. An event to "audit" the school/district can sound dry, but your job through the invitation is to build interest and commitment to the task; to develop understanding of how influential and important this work will be to learning; to give recognition to invitees for their past demonstration of leadership abilities; and to express the need for formal and informal leaders to share their talent at this time. Invitations can be made through personal conversations, phone calls, and letters, as well as through participation in established meetings such as PTA, school board, staff, and student government meetings.

3. You are now ready to plan the audit session. Think yummy food; think about a setting which lends itself to small and large group discussion; think comfortable chairs; think about a day and time when participants will be fresh and focused. I would plan for about a three-hour audit session.

4. Identify one person in each audit team who has the skills and abilities to facilitate a lively and inclusive professional discussion around the customized teaching and learning factors. Meet with the facilitators as a group prior to the audit session to make sure they are comfortable and prepared to lead a group using the audit tool in assessing the district/school relative to their assigned factor.

5. Distribute the rubric tool to all selected key stakeholders one week before the audit session. Ask them to read over the critical elements in their assigned factor and to begin thinking about how they would rate their school/district.

6. Begin the audit session with a quick review of all the customized teaching and learning factors. Be clear about the expected outcome for the session. Clarify roles of the group members. Watch the time and pace the group so each group member can be heard regarding her self-assessment of the school/district pursuant to their assigned factor. Encourage the groups to gather evidence and examples to justify their ratings. Allow time for each group to report their recommended rating, to receive feedback, and to answer questions from the large group. End the session with a communication regarding how the audit will be used to facilitate change.

7. Communicate the results of the audit to all stakeholders.

○ Story

When Chuck Schwahn and I worked together with a group of over 100 stakeholders, we quickly discovered that an elected faculty leader in the group was vehemently opposed to envisioning any change to the current educational system. He began to make comments to disrupt, dominate, and/or derail the agenda. I watched as Chuck took him aside and challenged him to "get on the bus" and participate in shaping the future of the organization or "get off the bus." Chuck's intervention was both timely and effective in engaging the individual in a more positive way.

I learned to be prepared to manage group dynamics in a proactive way. Dissenting viewpoints are an important part of any serious discussion. Disruptive, disrespectful, and unprofessional behavior is not!

○ Going Forward

The audit will provide valuable information for use in identifying and prioritizing goals toward customized teaching and learning. Remember to align both fiscal and human resources with the goals so that some early successes will be possible!

Customized Teaching and Learning Rubric

	EMERGENT	PROFICIENT	EXEMPLARY
LEADERSHIP (Leadership)	Leaders are effective agents of change who know how to involve everyone in the change process and intentionally prepare others for leadership opportunities. Leaders have articulated a district Mission, Vision, Guiding Principles, and Learner Outcomes through a stakeholder dialogue.	Leaders are future-focused visionaries and have the courage to take risks to improve conditions for learning. They foster an organizational culture that values and rewards student success, creativity, innovation, and high quality. They make decisions based upon the district's strategic plan and vision. Leaders can clearly communicate the vision of a customized delivery system for learning. They can describe how that vision impacts each staff member within the system.	Leaders empower global stakeholders as contributing members of an evolving and dynamic enterprise. They align culture, policies, and practices with the vision of a customized delivery system. Their work is emulated by other leaders.
LEARNING (Teaching and Learning)	The district's philosophy of learning is well grounded in a constructivist paradigm in which the learner is involved in the planning of his learning experiences. Educators have a common understanding of the research on motivation and engagement.	The learner plans for her learning experiences with the assistance of a school coach and a parent or guardian. Learning is viewed as relevant to the learner. The creation of new knowledge is valued. Learners are motivated and allowed to learn at their individual maximum pace.	The district's philosophy of learning is evolving based upon a social constructivist paradigm in which the district is recognized as a place to watch students and adults study, analyze, and debate relevant cultural, religious, economic, and global issues.
CURRICULUM	The curriculum is written in a learner outcome format. Target knowledge is identified and rubrics are developed for assessment. Learner outcomes and targets are placed online for access by all stakeholders.	Learner outcomes are aligned with the district's mission and exit learner outcomes. Subject matter is integrated and applied to real-life problems. Digital content is used for greater levels of inquiry, analysis, creativity, collaboration, and content production.	Teachers and leaders are future-focused trend trackers. Their study of the future allows them to update curriculum content as new and relevant content emerges. The design of the curriculum is continuously transformed through the use of technology systems.
INSTRUCTION	Learners are grouped and re-grouped for specific learning targets and grade level lines begin to blur. Seminars have been created for learner outcomes requiring interaction with a learning facilitator. Instruction has shifted to a focus on learning goals vs. activities and assignments.	Learner progress is tracked by specific Learning Goals/Targets, rather than by activities or assignments. A formative approach is used to calculate progress/grades which does not include zeroes or averaging. Technology is used at a maximum level to customize learning experiences matched to developmental levels, learning styles, strengths, and interests. Instructional technology allows for an in-depth analysis of tasks, learners, and context. Delivery of instruction is differentiated by learning outcomes through the use of mentoring, online courses, seminars, and large group meetings.	Targeted instruction is informed by the use of technology in a systematic and comprehensive manner. A significant percentage of learning takes place in authentic community settings and through the use of exemplary online learning resources and courses.
ASSESSMENT	Assessments are directly aligned to learner outcomes. Assessments are presented in multiple formats including project-based assignments, portfolios, and demonstrations. Assessments are available online for all stakeholders.	Technology tools are used to facilitate authentic assessment tasks in multiple formats to meet varying learner needs. Electronic portfolios are used to show a complete record of learning accomplishments by exit outcomes. Portfolios are accessible to parents, learning coaches, and teachers. Learner assessment data are consistently and effectively used to provide feedback to continuously improve learning results.	Assessment tasks are innovative and carried out in real-life contexts. Students perform exceptionally well when compared to students in other schools regionally, nationally, and internationally.

Human Resources	**STAKEHOLDERS**	Parents and community members are supportive of teachers and the school system. Stakeholders articulate and enthusiastically support the vision in order to make changes in their schools to meet student and societal needs.	The global community serves as a learning laboratory. Adults mentor learners, businesses open their facilities for learning, and business/school partnerships allow for authentic learning opportunities. Selected global community members engage in online forums with learners and staff.	Global stakeholders are not only involved in school activities and serve as resources, but are also engaged in the design and development of the curriculum and authentic assessment tasks.
	PERSONNEL	All employees are hired, empowered, and retained because of their passion for educating children and young adults. They are caring and respectful in their interactions and connect personally with learners. They continually advance their knowledge and professional skills. Educators know that learners learn in different ways and they are flexible regarding learning styles and learning rates. They have high expectations and standards for learners. There is a collaborative relationship between the Board of Education, the leadership team, teachers, and support staff.	Selection, supervision, and advancement of personnel are aligned with the district's customized learning beliefs, values, mission, and vision. A professional learning culture which encourages and supports innovation and risk taking permeates the district at all levels. Professional development is aligned with customized learning and based upon a needs assessment of the employees. Employees develop and commit to individual learning plans for the implementation of customized learning. Mentoring and peer coaching is provided for employees by skilled coaches.	A reward and incentive structure which supports customized learning is an integral part of the appraisal system for teachers and administrators. The reputation of the district for excellence, innovation, and work climate make it an attractive choice for recruiting and retaining talented individuals.
Technology Resources	**STRUCTURE**	Information and communication technology infrastructure, including hardware and software, is planned and supports emerging policies and practices. Scheduling technology for individual learners has been designed/acquired and implemented. Accountability technology for administrators has been designed/acquired and implemented. Some standardized instructional and helpdesk support is provided for teachers and administrators.	Instructional technology resources allow for customization to enhance teaching and learning. Instructional designers and multimedia developers support teachers in their teaching with technology and the building of curriculum repositories. Support is provided for the use of technology for customized administrative tasks such as registration, student record keeping, room scheduling, assessment, grading, and communication. The administrative systems are interconnected. A monitoring system exists to ensure quality in the uploading and sharing of teaching and learning resources.	An instructional technology plan exists which allows for changes as new tools emerge. The plan is flexible in allowing for fit to the context of each school setting and needs of learners. Hardware and software purchases are based upon situational analysis and anticipated future needs of stakeholders. Access to the technology infrastructure is 24/7 with appropriate security.
	TECHNOLOGY	Every student has access to a computer and the Internet. The technology resources are geared toward the development of 21st Century skills especially higher-order thinking, research, collaborative and creative skills. Classrooms have direct connectivity with adequate bandwidth. The Information Technology System allows for privacy-protected communication between teachers, parents, and students.	Curriculum can be accessed online 24/7. The System supports the development of personal learning plans (PLP) with active involvement of parents. The System makes it possible for school leaders to track the activities and locations of individual students throughout the day.	Anyone can learn anything from anywhere at anytime. Technology is fully integrated into instruction and used for research, planning, communication, and to collect and manage data to guide decisions and inform continuous improvement. The use of technology has changed the teaching and learning process and improved student achievement, particularly in the full range of 21st Century skills.

Reference: Ping. C., Sing. C., & Churchill, D. (2010). *Leading ICT in educational practices: A capacity building toolkit for teacher education institutions in the Asia-Pacific.* Singapore: Microsoft Partners in Learning.

A BOOK STUDY FOR GROWING A SHARED VISION

by James D. Parry

○ Connection to *inevitable*

Clearly, the foremost message of *inevitable* is about creating a vision for Mass Customized Learning (MCL). In Chapter 10, Chuck and Bea emphasize the leader's role in "creating, communicating, and 'selling' the MCL vision." They speak to the five leadership domains as defined by Schwahn and Spady in their work titled ***Total Leaders***. Visionary Leadership, one of the domains, portrays leaders "who describe a concrete picture of change . . . and help everyone understand how the change will affect him personally." A book study is highlighted as one strategy for leaders to engage stakeholders with ideas and information that increases awareness and builds understanding leading to a shared vision for MCL.

Frankly, I am a bit embarrassed about the term "book study." The term may conjure up an image of stodgy folks gathered in a circle with a thick volume in their laps more than a picture of education stakeholders energized by online discussion. Despite the old terminology, a book study that reflects a 21st Century context may be a powerful starting point for building a shared vision for customized learning with stakeholders. Whether the preferred venue for the book study is face-to-face or online, a thoughtful, engaging study holds much potential for healthy dialogue for moving stakeholders forward in their thinking in a manner fitting with the authors of *inevitable*.

○ Primary Topic

Leadership, Teaching and Learning, Human Resources, Technology Resources

○ Primary Audience

This is a resource for school leaders initiating a systemic change process in schools and requiring buy-in across a diversity of education stakeholders. Leaders need to consider the context of their respective schools or districts and the intended outcome of the activity to determine the target audience for their book studies. In many cases, the target audience will be decision-makers such as school board members. As leaders build support for the change, the target audience may encompass teachers, parents, or community members. The key is being deliberate about engaging a diversity of stakeholders as part of a developing, thoughtful process to build an informed base of support for implementing and sustaining the change.

○ Purpose

A book study is a relatively low investment and potentially high pay-off activity for engaging stakeholders in meaningful and productive discussions about current issues. In this case, the book study is designed to engage stakeholders (teachers, administrators, boards of education, students, parents, and/or community members) in dialogue about the "reality" of their schools and the potential of MCL for their students. As stakeholders invest in the study, they grow to embrace the opportunity that customized learning presents and get on board with a systemic change process for their schools.

○ Rationale

Book studies are a common activity among progressive educators, especially within professional learning communities (PLCs). Such studies afford groups of stakeholders the opportunity to explore and examine topics of importance and relevance to the education community. While informally-structured book studies can be effective, a more formal approach with clear outcomes and a carefully designed process leads to greater impact.

A literature search produces a variety of examples for designing and implementing book studies. A common theme is that the role of the leader and facilitator is critical. Foremost, they need to ensure that participants are valued as respected contributors to the conversations. Another critical variable is thoughtful discussion questions. Often, the questions are noted as the key to meaningful group dialogue that is inclusive and productive. Book study champions contend that a strong leader with the right questions is a good starting point for positive results. Also, they advocate book studies as powerful stretching and learning opportunities for addressing change issues in schools; that is, a change such as that engendered by the vision of MCL.

○ Process for Use

Let's start the description of the book study process with a couple of assumptions. First of all, we will assume the obvious. You are interested in this book study because it is about *inevitable* and the vision of MCL. Secondly, it is assumed that you are in a leadership position and you will take the lead role for designing, facilitating, and assessing the book study. Certainly, you will engage peers or colleagues as teammates in the process. Your teammates serve both as *collaborators* in planning a strong process and *sounding boards* as you reflect upon and check your perceptions. By keeping your perceptions informed, you are positioned for better judgments for steering the book study positively as it unfolds.

In the following paragraphs you will find the description of a step-by-step process to serve as a resource for school leaders. If you are an experienced leader and facilitator, you may choose to skip right to the suggested reflection questions at the end of this resource. For those leaders preferring more guidance, you may want to scan the following information to be reminded of key aspects of a thoughtful book study. And for those leaders who desire a more comprehensive description of the elements essential to a successful book study, you may choose to delve into the four components laid out in the next few pages.

As we launch into the description of the process, I wish for you to know that I work with a progressive organization that embraces and models the use of technology. So what? Well, we like to practice what we preach. In this case, we have current experience conducting book studies in two venues, face-to-face and online. Just as the theme of MCL is about fitting learning to the needs of learners, you will want to choose the venue for the book study that is the best fit for the participants and context of the school. Many aspects of an effective book study such as a clear purpose may be the same whether the discussion is conducted face-to-face or online. However, as the book study process is described below, nuances about the two venues are noted. Describing the nuances is intended to help you make more informed decisions about the best venue or combination of venues for your audience and for your purposes.

1. **Be clear about the purpose of the *Inevitable* book study.** The first step in designing the book study is clarifying the purpose. As a school leader, you are already energized by the vision of MCL. You are eager for others to share your enthusiasm. However, enthusiasm must be balanced with clarity about the purpose for engaging in a book study. Toward that end, key questions to ask yourself are:
   a. What is to be accomplished?
   b. Who are the target audience or participants given the purpose?
   c. Why is the book study a good strategy for the stated purpose?
   Example of purpose: *Through engaging in a book study of **inevitable**, a key group of board of education members and teacher leaders will embrace the MCL vision and will support initiatives which align with that vision.*

2. **Identify the target audience for the *inevitable* book study.** In part, there is a "chicken-and-egg" dynamic at play here. The purpose and audience are interdependent so you will be thinking about the audience at the same time you are clarifying the purpose. Recognizing that you are at the start of a school change process about customized learning, you will want to be deliberate about gaining buy-in of key stakeholders. Key questions for you include:
   a. Who are the stakeholders or stakeholder groups for whom buy-in is critical if this systemic change is to be embraced and implemented?
   b. What are the current perceptions of key stakeholders about systemic school change?
   c. Who among the stakeholders are persons of influence who could serve as leaders and levers for other stakeholders?
   Example of target audience: *A key group of teacher leaders and board of education members are identified as the target audience for the **inevitable** book study because the teacher leader*

group is respected and valued as "movers-and-shakers" among their peers and the board of education has a track record of responding supportively to the practical and credible voice of the teacher leaders.

3. **Design and implement the *inevitable* book study.** With a clear purpose and target audience noted, you shift your focus to design and implementation. An investment in planning pays dividends in terms of the quality of the study experience and probability of the desired outcomes. At a minimum, the plan and implementation should address the following factors.

   a. **Identify the venue for the book study.** That is, should the study be designed as a face-to-face activity, an online experience, or a blended learning activity? Questions to guide that decision include:

      i. Will a face-to-face, online, or blended venue accomplish or contribute to the purpose of the book study most effectively? Why? (While all three venues may achieve the purpose, might engaging stakeholders with an online discussion experience serve to build their awareness of such technology tools? Or, would the importance of face-to-face interaction outweigh the potential value of an online experience?)

      ii. How do the variables of cost (travel expense associated with attending book study sessions) or time (long commutes associated with the site of book study) influence participation and thereby impact the choice of venue?

      iii. How do the individual schedules of participants accommodate or preclude a face-to-face venue? An online venue?

      iv. How do relationships among the target audience members influence the choice of venue? (Keep reading as the next topic is the importance of relationship among participants. Observations about current relationships may influence the decision about the venue for the book study.)

   Example of venue choice: *Given the busy schedules and great travel distances for the target audience (board of education members and teacher leaders), the venue for the book study will be online. Recognizing the technical nature of an online study, an initial face-to-face session is scheduled for the target audience members to meet the other study participants and to acquaint them with the asynchronous online discussion system.*

   b. **Initiate or affirm a level of relationship among the study group members to encourage trust and active participation**. Clearly, the mantra "relationship, relationship, relationship" applies here. Respectful relationships among the target audience members are essential for maximizing the book study opportunity. Questions to consider as you reflect on relationships are:

      i. Do the stakeholders comprising the target audience have established relationships? If so, how are those relationships perceived? Based on those perceptions, how might relationships be enhanced?

ii. Or, is this the first time a significant number of the stakeholders have interacted? If so, how might relationships be initiated or encouraged?

Example of attention to relationship: *To initiate productive relationships among a target audience of teacher leaders and board of education members prior to an online book study, the group is brought together for a face-to-face session. The agenda for the session is designed to:*

i. Provide an overview of the book study process.

ii. Engage the participants in an introductory activity so they meet others. For example, ask the participants to move around the room and share with another person or two their responses to a stage set such as: *Reflect on a major change you experienced (job change, relocation, etc.). What was a particularly challenging or stretching aspect of that change? What was a learning you took from that change process?*

iii. Demonstrate the online discussion system that participants will use for the book study discussion so there is a shared comfort level with a venue that may be new to some participants.

b **Identify and communicate the schedule, format, and norms for participation in the *inevitable* book study**. In a nutshell, the purpose for the book study is "what" is to be accomplished and the schedule, format, and norms address "how" it is accomplished. While serendipity may work at moments, the most productive book studies happen when leaders pay attention to implementation concerns such as schedule, format, and norms.

i **Schedule**. Dealing with busy folks always makes scheduling a challenge. However, being explicit so participants can note dates and times well in advance is one strategy to encourage regular participation. If individual schedules magnify the challenge of scheduling the book study, leaders may want to give the online venue serious consideration. Because the typical online discussion is asynchronous, participants would have the flexibility to participate in the book study at a time that works best for them.

Example of an *inevitable* face-to-face book study schedule: *The book study is scheduled to begin during the first week of the fall term and will focus on one chapter per session. The study group will meet on the first and third Wednesdays of the month from 5:00 – 6:30 PM for a five-month period. Snacks will be provided.*

Example of an *inevitable* online book study schedule: *The book study is scheduled to begin during the first week of the fall term and will focus on one chapter for each session. The book study will run for five months with a two-week discussion window for each chapter. Reflection questions for the identified chapter will be posted in two-week intervals beginning with the first Wednesday of the month. Participants will post and read responses; that is, engage in asynchronous online dialogue throughout each two-week period. (Virtual snacks or perhaps a gift card to a local coffee shop with free internet access)*

  i. **Format.** For building awareness or shared understanding for a target audience of education stakeholders, a simple discussion format in response to a few thoughtful reflection questions and guided by you in your facilitator role is a productive activity. Such questions are critical to focus dialogue in either the face-to-face or online venue. Suggested reflection questions for each chapter of ***inevitable*** are included as an addendum to this resource.

  ii. **Norms.** Effective group processes include establishing norms which set expectations for participation. In particular, norms can shape the behavior of participants to encourage respectful discourse and value input from all of the participants. Communicating and clarifying the norms as the book study begins sets the tone for future sessions. Also, having the group norms established upfront empowers you to function in more of a "reminder" role than a "reprimanding" role regarding participant interactions.

Example of group norms for a <u>face-to-face</u> venue: *In order to maximize the **inevitable** book study discussion time, participants agree to honor the following norms: Be consistent in attendance. Stay focused on the topic. No distracting side conversations. Do not interrupt others. Encourage participation from everyone. Be constructive. It is okay to disagree. Be open-minded and listen to the observations of others.*

Example of group norms for an <u>online</u> venue: *In order to maximize the **inevitable** book study discussion time, participants agree to honor the following norms: Stay focused on the topic in your responses and feedback. Take side conversations offline. Encourage others' participation. Be constructive. It is okay to disagree. Be open-minded as you read the observations of others.*

4. **Assess the impact of the book study.** As book studies wrap up, it is important for you to reflect on the process and the results. Potential questions include: How well did the book study achieve the intended purpose? Were there unintended outcomes that should be noted? Equally important, how did the book study process work for the participants? How did the process work for you in your facilitator role? What was learned? Whether you simply reflect on the questions from your own perceptions or whether you gather data from others, investing energy in assessing the impact is time well spent. It is wise to capture and record the information from the assessment so it can serve as data for next steps. If the book study achieved its purpose, more stakeholders are energized about the vision of MCL. With increased energy comes more momentum. As a result, you have developed more partners for engaging in more steps toward the shared vision. And a "simple" book study played a vital role in that progress!

As the leader/facilitator, you perform a critical role from start to finish. Clearly, that role requires a commitment of your time and energy. One of the most crucial times is your role during the group discussion portion of the study. During that part of study, whether the venue is face-to-face or online, you need to take the lead in a deliberate and focused manner. The following list adapted from the work of Kelsey and Plumb[1] is helpful for leaders:

- Keep the group focused.
- Demonstrate a perspective that serves the whole group rather than individuals.
- Own your bias.
- Reflect an objectivity that serves the group process.
- Encourage everyone to participate.
- Model listening in the face-to-face or reading in the online venue.
- Address conflict and guide parties by negotiating shared understanding, even agreeing to disagree.
- Adapt the process as appropriate on the fly.
- Summarize status of discussion by noting consensus or diversity.

Clearly, your attention to those specific responsibilities will earn the respect of the participants and heighten the impact of the book study.

◎ Story

A couple of colleagues who are leaders in small rural districts in the Midwest are facilitating face-to-face book studies about *inevitable*. Both chose to start with their boards of education and they are gaining momentum. In one district, the study generated so much energy among the board members that teachers suggested that they, too, be involved in a book study as a next step. Furthermore, the school leader in that district reports that the interest is spreading to the community. In rural areas where the school is a primary hub of community news, word of something new or different spreads quickly. As a result, the school leader anticipates that a community-wide awareness session addressing the vision of MCL is a logical next step.

While there is significant interest in the other small district, budgetary constraints are influencing the perceptions of some board members. The school leader engaged the board in a candid discussion about fiscal issues. With that reality thoughtfully acknowledged, board members were able to resume a more productive discussion about the potential of customized learning. Clearly, the insight of the school leader regarding human dynamics and group process contributed to the positive outcome and set a constructive onramp for future study sessions.

In both of these small rural communities, the school leadership is respected and stable. As a result, there is a foundation of trust in the schools and communities which is essential when introducing a system change such as MCL. For these leaders, a face-to-face book study was a comfortable and effective strategy for building awareness.

During this same time period, Technology and Innovation in Education (TIE) offered interested folks from the broader statewide education community the opportunity to participate in an online book study about *Inevitable*. The purpose was the same as the face-to-face study; that is, growing awareness and support for the vision of MCL. The book study was open to any interested educators across the state and it attracted participants in a diversity of roles from special educator to third grade teacher to teacher aide. Designed as a four-week experience, the facilitator posted new reflection questions twice a week. During the first week, participants were asked to introduce themselves with a short description about their professional role along with something about themselves personally. Typically, participants would get online two or three times a week to post their responses and make observations about the responses of others. As in a face-to-face discussion, one participant's comments were fodder for another's. The facilitator checked in daily to ensure broad-based participation, make connections among comments, challenge viewpoints, and summarize the discussion.

A perusal of the online dialogue indicates that participants are comfortable enough to be frank and open about their thinking. An offline visit with the participants affirms that some are inclined to be more candid in online discussion as compared to sitting face-to-face with others. Some participants noted how much they valued the opportunity to develop their understanding of MCL in somewhat anonymous groups so they felt better equipped for face-to-face conversations with stakeholders in their own districts.

Clearly, the nuances between the face-to-face venue and the online venue are significant and both have demonstrated value. The key for leaders is discerning which venue or combination of venues is the best fit for their purpose and their contexts.

○ Going Forward

As *inevitable* and the power of the MCL vision capture more attention in the education community, I anticipate many school leaders will capitalize on the potential of books studies. Contextual factors vary across school communities so the stories stemming from book studies will vary as well. As powerful stories are discovered, they will be captured so they might be shared for the benefit of the larger education community.

○ Reference

[1]Kelsey, D., & Plumb, P. (2003). *Great meetings! How to facilitate like a pro.* Portland, ME: Hanson Park Press.

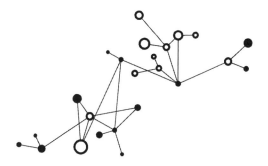

Inevitable BOOK STUDY TOOL

by James D. Parry

Involving book study participants with discussion questions which engage and energize is a key to a productive study. Clearly, the questions should align with the outcome that the leadership has in mind for the study. At the same time, the questions should be stated in a manner that invites diverse responses and encourages a rich discussion. The following questions are offered as a starter set to stimulate and assist leaders with identifying questions that fit with the context of their respective studies.

○ Chapter 1: *Facing Reality*

- From your perspective, which *stage* of the change process as captured on pages 3 - 4 reflects the perception of folks in your school community? What is the basis for your perception?
- As you consider the *harsh realities*, which statement do you believe is the most challenging for stakeholders in your school community to accept? Why?
- As you focus on your particular school or district, what other *harsh realities* come to mind? Why do you think this harsh reality is unique to your school community?
- As you consider the list labeled *what we do that doesn't make sense anymore* found on pages 7 - 11, which items stir the greatest reaction from you? Why?
- Based on what we know about the role of intrinsic motivation (pages 12 - 13) with learning and the power of current technologies, the stage is set for big changes in education. What needs to happen next in your school community to move toward such change?

Chapter 2: *The Future Is Now: Transformational Technologies*

- What strikes you about Chuck's mass customized day as captured on pages 21 - 24? Do you think he is an anomaly? Why or why not?
- As the matrix on the bottom of page 24 suggests, *empowerment* has shifted from top-down to more of a bottom-up perspective where the voices of individuals tend to be valued more. What examples or evidence of that shift come to mind for you? In business, government, communities, or schools?
- On page 25, the authors offer numerous examples reflecting the potential of technology to address an "individual" level of interaction and response. Where and how have you experienced this level of interaction and response via technology? From your perspective, what value do you believe the application of these technologies offers education? What do you see as barriers to the application of these technologies?

Chapter 3: *But First...Our Purpose*

- In a sentence, how would you define the purpose of *school* in your community? In what ways is it apparent that your school or district gets learners ready for life? Ready for more school? How do you perceive the balance between *life preparation* and *more-schooling preparation*?
- As you consider the strategic design questions noted on pages 42 - 51, do you perceive that your school community is poised to address such questions? Why or why not?
- As you reflect on the exit learner outcomes listed on page 48, what strikes you? In your opinion, which outcomes are learners in your school community best prepared to demonstrate? What would you note as the biggest gaps for learners in your school community? Why?

Chapter 4: *Through the Learner's Eyes*

- How would you describe the differences between the *digital natives* and *digital immigrants* in your school community? How do those differences affect relationships? What could the school community do to enhance shared understanding and stronger relationships?
- On pages 59 – 65, the authors share a scenario about Lori's school day. How is her day similar or different from high school students in your school district? The authors add the nuances of a learner such as Johnny on pages 67 – 69. Currently, how is your school addressing the needs of learners such as Johnny? From your perspective, are Johnny's needs being addressed as needed? Why or why not?
- On pages 71 - 72, Chuck shares a story about two brothers; actually, his brother and himself. One enjoyed his life work and the other did not. Undoubtedly, you can relate personally or know someone who fits the story. How well do you think learners in your school community get connected to their *passions*? Why do you think that is the situation? What role might the school community play in helping learners connect to their passions?

○ Chapter 5: *About Learning: The Baby and the Bathwater*

- Chuck and Bea present the *baby and bathwater* metaphor to address concerns associated with major changes in education. The discussion is summed up with the matrix on the bottom of page 79. They conclude by stating that *you don't throw out bathwater because it is bathwater, rather you throw out bathwater when you have better bathwater*. Do you buy their logic? Why or why not?

- On page 82, Chuck and Bea list the *Top Ten Babies*. Do you find that you are agreeing with the list? Why or why not? As you think about your school or district, are there *babies* that you would add?

- The first four *babies* noted on pages 82 – 89 address motivation. How well do you think the teaching and learning in your school develops intrinsic motivation in learners? What would you recommend for strengthening efforts regarding intrinsic motivation?

○ Chapter 6: *MCL: The Vision (Detailed)*

- Chuck and Bea contend that for a vision to be powerful, it needs to "run well ahead of the organization's present capacity to do them." They believe that visions should *pull* rather than *push* people, teams, or organizations. How well does the vision of your school leaders fit with that perspective? Why or why not?

- Pursuing the bold vision of Mass Customized Learning requires a new vocabulary. It means loosening our grip on some comfortable terms such as *students, grade levels, and classes* and embracing terms such as *learners, learner outcomes, and learning opportunities*. How comfortable is that shift for you and your colleagues? Why? Why do you think such a shift is so important?

- On pages 104 – 113, the authors share the strategic design efforts of the Sycamore Community School District. Could you see your school community doing such significant work? Why or why not? What would you propose as the next steps for your school community towards developing or maintaining a bold vision?

○ Chapter 7: *Lori Does Her Learning Plan/Schedule*

- A short video titled *Lori schedules her learning plan* is accessible at http://youtu.be/xdCHvLSR_Iw. The video offers a visual image of the Lori scenario found on pages 119-127. What strikes you about Lori's experience? How is the scheduling process for Lori similar or different from the process at your school?

- Clearly, Lori is a fairly mature teenager with parent support which contributes to her success. It is tougher to visualize disadvantaged learners being successful. Describe the learners in your school community who face the greatest disadvantages. How might those learners be supported and supervised to encourage their success with the scheduling process reflected in the video?

- This chapter wraps up on pages 128 -129 by raising challenging questions about the *purpose of education* and the *degree of control in education*. Frankly, there is no absolute answer for these questions. In reality, learners come in all "shapes and sizes." As a result, some need more structure while others benefit from more flexibility. A Mass Customized delivery system can enhance teaching and learning regardless of the philosophy about purpose and control. From your perspective, how well are school leaders in your community able to reach compromise about philosophy so that your school is able to move forward with the potential of Mass Customized Learning? How would you articulate the position of your school community regarding these philosophical issues?

○ Chapter 8: *Weight Bearing Walls (WBWs)*

- What makes you anxious or excited about moving the WBWs noted on pages 136 - 140?
- From your perspective, which of the WBWs are most challenging to move in your school community? Why?
- From your perspective, which stakeholder group (students, teachers, administrators, board members, parents, community members, others?) will struggle the most with the implications of moving WBWs? Why?
- Which of the WBWs offer the greatest opportunities to enhance learning? Why? How would you suggest pursuing such an opportunity in your school community?

○ Chapter 9: *Ready for Rollout*

- This chapter emphasizes critical elements, or infrastructure, that need to be in place as a school community implements the MCL vision. Seven specific elements are listed on page 146. The first several elements are less dependent on technological infrastructure while the subsequent elements require sophisticated technological infrastructure. As you consider this list, how do you perceive your school in regards to *ready for rollout* for implementing MCL? What causes you to have that perception?
- On pages 148 -149, Chuck and Bea offer a list of learning format options. As you review that list, which format options already are available in your school? If some are not available, how might those options be made available at your school?
- To fully implement the MCL vision requires sophisticated technology systems which empower learners, teachers, and administrators. One component of such a system was reflected in the video titled *Lori schedules her learning plan*. How capable is your school's current technology infrastructure for implementing elements of the MCL vision such as scheduling? What needs to happen to improve the capability of your school's technology infrastructure? How might those needs be addressed?

○ Chapter 10: *Total Leaders*

- Repeatedly, education literature has affirmed leadership as a key to meaningful school change. This chapter is filled with insights about the type of leadership that is essential to productive change. In short, the authors identify two broad responsibilities for leadership: 1) setting the organization's direction, and 2) creating the organizational alignment that will effectively move the organization in that direction. As a stakeholder in your school community, how clear are you regarding your school's direction and alignment? Do you perceive that there is a shared understanding of the direction and alignment in your school community? From your perspective, what might enhance clarity? What might enhance alignment?

- From your perspective, is the leadership direction and alignment congruent with the MCL vision? If so, in what ways is it congruent? If not, what might make it more congruent?

◎ Chapter 11: The Elementary MCL Vision

- On a scale of 1 to 10 with 10 being fully ready, how would you rate the readiness of your school community (learners, parents, teachers, and administrators) for the elementary school structure described in this chapter? Who is most ready or least ready? What data or experiences support your observations about the readiness of your school community?

- As you reflect on Lincoln's comments (2nd edition: page 186) about his school experience, how do you think the perspective of learners attending your elementary school would be similar or different? What data or experiences support your observation?

- Integrating technology as a tool was vital to restructuring at West Elementary School. As you reflect on the use of technology at your elementary school, how is it similar or different from West Elementary School? From your perspective, how might your elementary school address technology integration to move forward with the vision of MCL?

- The teacher team at West Elementary School applied a new lens to facilitating learning at their school. For example, they grouped and regrouped learners in thoughtful, deliberate ways to enhance the learning experience. As you reflect on the strategies and processes that the teacher team implemented (2nd edition: pages 205-210), what strikes you as most compelling? From your perspective, how might such an approach have value for your elementary school and its learners?

◎ Chapter 12: *What's In It For You (WIIFYs)?*

- By this point, the authors presume that readers recognize that MCL is indeed inevitable. They hope you have been energized by the potential of MCL and the opportunity to be a part of the change process. Toward that end, they highlight WIIFYs for various stakeholders (1st edition: pages 184-187; 2nd edition: pages 218-221). As you review the highlights, what strikes you as most compelling and most urgent?

- A part of the authors' strategy is to engage the education community, and they have established a website at www.masscustomizedlearning.com. At the website, you can access short interviews with the Chuck and Bea. As you view those video clips, what strikes you about their observations and comments? Having read and considered *inevitable*, what observations and feedback would you have for Chuck and Bea?

SCHOOLS ON THE MOVE WITH CUSTOMIZATION: EXAMPLES

by John Swanson and James D. Parry

◎ Connection to *inevitable*

The vision of MCL is so compelling. And, schools are so institutionalized. That is where we find ourselves, isn't it? Yet, intent on moving toward customized teaching and learning, progressive schools around the country are initiating changes that challenge the traditional school structure. Often referred to as blended learning, these initiatives strive to meet more individual learner needs in a manner that stretches, even alters, the familiar school structure. In general, blended learning is—well, blended. Learners still experience some fairly traditional classroom instruction. At the same time, that instruction is blended or complemented by instruction that is more innovative. Virtually all blended learning initiatives incorporate technology as a tool for the teaching and learning process. All in all, a blended learning approach puts schools on a path toward the vision of MCL.

◎ Primary Topic

Leadership, Teaching and Learning, Human Resources, Technology Resources

◎ Primary Audience

It is beneficial and powerful for ALL stakeholders to gain awareness of initiatives in schools across the country to embrace and engage in aspects of customized teaching and learning.

◎ Purpose

The purpose of this resource is: 1) To provide examples of blended learning initiatives that might spur ideas among a team of education leaders and stakeholders, and 2) To offer examples of questions that teams might consider as they clarify and focus a blended learning initiative. The examples and questions serve as a catalyst for engaging team members in a directed, productive discussion about others' efforts as a springboard for talking about possibilities for their own initiative.

◎ Rationale

Educators and education leaders feel the growing tension between the compelling vision of MCL and the institutionalization of the traditional school structure. Progressive education stakeholders are determined to invest their energy in restructuring schools so they are learner-centered, consequently, they capitalize on the robust tools of the 21st Century so powerfully embraced by the world around us. As convinced as most stakeholders are, many are uncertain about their next steps. Many of the traditional school structures, or weight bearing walls (WBWs) as labeled by Chuck and Bea, need to be replaced. Yet action on all of them at the same time is simply unrealistic. As a result, leaders of blended learning initiatives are demonstrating the wisdom of a focused approach which implements changes to selected school structures in meaningful ways. In short, these leaders identify avenues for ramping in to the MCL vision. Once successfully ramped in, the blended learning initiatives can expand and tackle more school structures requiring change. This fieldbook resource shares examples of blended learning initiatives and suggests questions that stakeholders can use for focusing their energies and ramping in to the MCL vision.

◎ Process for Use

As teams of education stakeholders come together to make progress with the vision of MCL, they can ground and accelerate their efforts by valuing the work and learning of others invested in blended learning initiatives. Toward that end, the following examples are offered as a resource and catalyst for stakeholders starting a journey toward customized teaching and learning. The examples span k-12 blended learning initiatives. Some initiatives reflect a "gentle" approach with limited, but important, changes to traditional school structures. Others reflect a more aggressive approach with significant changes to familiar school structures. Hopefully, the brief introductions to these initiatives challenge the team of stakeholders to delve more deeply in learning about current initiatives. As a result, their discussion will be rich and relevant and help them clarify the next steps for their own blended learning initiative.

◎ Overarching Questions

As a team begins the process of identifying a focus for their work, a few big questions serve as a guide. The obvious, but critical, question is: What is the focus of our blended learning initiative? That is, what need, problem, or opportunity are we addressing and why are we addressing it? Also, where do we have energy, enthusiasm, or momentum which offers us our best opportunity for change? Finally, how might we align resources to facilitate the potential of our initiative? Coming back to these overarching questions as a reference point for team discussions will help the discussion stay grounded in key issues and considerations. Now, on to the examples.

◎ Example A:

Leading Question: *How might a blended learning initiative effectively address the priority of individual learner needs or subgroups of learners?*

Initiative: Cyber Village Academy is a 3rd through 12th grade charter school in St. Paul, Minnesota, which offers a blended on-campus and online approach to education. While particular instructional options may vary somewhat based on grade level, the three programs offered by the academy "are tailored to meet students' needs, supporting and challenging them at their unique point of growth." In part, the academy uses technology to expand educational opportunities and accomplish their mission with learners and families. Depending on the grade level of the student, the academy's schedule engages learners with online experiences at home two or three days and with on-campus learning activities the remaining two or three days of the week.

The Cyber Village Academy started in the late 90s as a school using technology to meet the academic needs of chronically ill students and has evolved into a blended learning community serving a broad range of students from across the Twin Cities and surrounding area. It is a powerful example of starting with a focus on service to a subgroup of students and expanding to serve many learners.

Link: http://www.cybervillageacademy.org/

⊙ Example B:

Leading Question: *How might a blended learning initiative effectively address the unique needs of a subgroup of learners?*

Initiative: Launched in 2008 through support from the National Math and Science Initiative (NMSI), Learning Power is a statewide program providing Advanced Placement (AP) courses in mathematics, science, and English for students in small, rural high schools via an online delivery system. Typical students in the program participate in one or two Learning Power courses and receive the remainder of their coursework locally in face-to-face classrooms. In its fourth year of operation, several hundred students from 60 rural high schools across South Dakota asynchronously access Learning Power content presented by some of the state's finest teachers. The asynchronous component is enhanced with online discussion groups and one-to-one teacher to student online interactions for day-to-day support. Each student receives the support of a local educator, referred to as an e-mentor, who serves as an encourager for the learner and a connector with the online teacher as appropriate. The percentage of Learning Power students achieving qualifying scores on College Board exams is comparable to face-to-face learners in the state. Particularly notable is the success of students in courses with lab components such as AP Chemistry, AP Biology, and AP Physics. In general, the labs are a combination of virtual, hands-on, and video-based lab activities.

Learning Power serves students who previously had almost no access to AP opportunities. Because of rural, isolated demographics, practically none of the small high schools has the critical mass of students or qualified teaching staff to make AP courses available to interested and capable learners. As a result, Learning Power is addressing an important subgroup of learners in a manner which positions these students for increased success at postsecondary institutions.

Link: http://learningpower.tie.net/default.htm

○ Example C:

Leading Question*: How might a blended learning initiative effectively address a priority of keeping high risk learners from dropping out or seeking other education providers?*

Initiative: Infinity Cyber Academy is a grade 6-12 program of the Quakertown Community School District in Pennsylvania. The academy provides online courses in core subject areas as an alternative to face-to-face classes. The program affords students the flexibility to fit courses into their work schedules, complete courses at their own pace, and stay on the path to graduation.

Launched in 2008, the academy was started with the hope of keeping high-risk students from dropping out, providing flexibility for students with outside-of-school commitments, and supporting students wishing to accelerate. The program is growing dramatically and serves as a successful strategy for one level of customization.

Link: http://www.qcsd.org/infinity/site/default.asp

○ Example D:

Leading Question: *How might a blended learning approach effectively address a priority of being at the forefront of innovation or well-founded school change?*

Initiative: The Michigan Virtual School (MVS) provides online courses in core subject areas to interested grade 6-12 students and schools. It affords learners the opportunity to increase their course and scheduling options. The typical student takes an MVS course from a remote location while attending a traditional middle or high school for their other coursework. MVS's delivery model offers three levels of student-teacher interaction: a) *Instructor-led* courses are conducted in a virtual environment but reflect the student experience of a traditional classroom; b) *Instructor-less* courses are a fit for highly independent learners and offer almost no instructor involvement; and c) *Instructor-supported* courses are the newest option providing teacher support to answer questions, but assignments and exams are auto-scored.

The impetus for MVS stemmed from legislative action in the late 90's to establish a catalyst for change for strengthening teaching and learning in K-12. Subsequently, MVS was launched and has evolved into a vital service provider of high quality, cost-effective online courses. Most recently, MVS is playing a change agent role in the area of teacher development in Michigan.

Link: http://www.mivhs.org/

⊙ Example E:

Leading Question: *How might a blended learning approach help us make better use of available instructional time?*

Initiative: Rocketship Education is an expanding network of grade K-5 elementary schools originating in San Jose, California. In particular, the model is focused on increasing student achievement of disadvantaged students in high need communities. Students spend twenty-five percent of their time online in a learning lab where reading and mathematics instruction is focused on individual learning needs and skills practice. Seventy-five percent of the school day is spent in classrooms where face-to-face teachers emphasize concept extension and the development of critical thinking skills. Rocketship leaders have blended online and face-to-face interactions for learners by shifting the daily schedule to make progress with customizing teaching and learning for individual student needs.

Link: http://www.rsed.org/

⊙ Example F:

Leading Question: *How might a blended learning approach shift the roles and responsibilities of teachers in order to produce more self-directed learners?*

Initiative: Carpe Diem Collegiate High School and Middle School (CDCHS) offers core subjects to secondary students in a unique, accredited campus experience or online experience from its Yuma, Arizona location. The on-campus program affords learners access to onsite teacher-facilitators and computer-assisted instruction. The online program offers "anytime-anyplace" access to courses along with real time, online support via Student Support Centers. The program reflects the philosophy that all students should receive a high quality experience and technology-based education designed to help them be successful today, tomorrow, and in the future.

In 2002, CDCHS opened as a traditional high school in rented facilities. When that location was no longer available, school leaders capitalized on the opportunity to transition to an innovative blended model. Now they operate in a building that was designed for their blended approach. During the day, students rotate for two or three cycles between a one-to-one computer lab where much of the content is presented and face-to-face classrooms where the content is enhanced or applied. A part of the CDCHS campus model is an innovative staffing pattern. In a building with a capacity of 300 students, six full-time certified teachers for the core subjects serve as coaches during the face-to-face classroom time. There is only one teacher for each subject area—with significantly increased compensation for these teachers reflective of their critical roles. During the online instruction periods, highly qualified paraprofessionals, referred to as assistant coaches, provide support for the students. CDCHS is invested directly and successfully in the issue of shifting roles of teachers and maximizing resources.

Link: http://carpediemschools.com/

◯ Example G:

Leading Question: *Which of the core subject areas might afford us the best opportunity for gaining experience with blended learning?*

Initiative: Recently in Stillwater, Minnesota, the public school system implemented a "flipped classroom" pilot program for mathematics instruction in grades 4-6. After each school day, students watch asynchronous videos online of math lessons created and presented by local teachers. Then the students complete a short quiz of comprehensive questions. At school the next day, they practice and apply their learning in a classroom with a face-to-face teacher. The data from the daily quizzes inform the practice and application activities implemented in the classroom. District leaders believe the pilot holds much potential for customizing teaching and learning in the future.

A review of numerous blended learning initiatives indicates that the choice of mathematics as the target subject area is the most common. In addition to the Stillwater project, other examples with a mathematics focus include the Khan Academy Collaborative Partnership. (http://www.innosightinstitute.org/blended-learning-2/los-altos-school-district/) and the School of One described later in this resource.

Link: http://www.innosightinstitute.org/blended-learning-2/blprofiles-innosight/stillwater-area-public-schools/

◯ Resource of Blended Learning Examples

A key resource for more blended learning examples is accessible at a link of the Innosight Institute (http://www.innosightinstitute.org/media-room/publications/blended-learning/blended-learning-profiles-all-profiles/). The Innosight Institute is a not-for-profit think tank working to apply Harvard Business School Professor Clayton M. Christensen's theories of disruptive innovation. Their intent is to develop and promote solutions for social issues including challenges in education.

◯ Story

During our research for blended learning examples, we discovered the School of One. It is an example and a powerful model. As a result, it is timely to share their story as another catalyst for stakeholders wanting to make progress with the vision of MCL.

When it comes to middle school mathematics, the School of One embraces key components of the vision of MCL. Launched in selected middle schools in New York City with the support of partners, the concept engages learners in a range of "modalities" based on their needs. Modalities range from group instruction to small group collaboration to individualized virtual instruction or tutoring to independent practice with traditional materials such as workbooks. Teachers provide facilitation and support for learners along the way.

The School of One concept depends on a schedule that makes time for mathematics instruction a priority and a sophisticated technology "engine" which works behind the scenes to guide the instructional process based on learner needs. School of One students participate in a double dose of mathematics with two morning periods each day designated for their math instruction. Also, students complete an online mini-assessment each day. The assessment data feed into an algorithm which produces a daily customized learning plan for each learner, referred to as a "playlist."

The playlist reflects the learner's instructional focus and activity for the day as well as informs the teachers' role in the process. For example, the daily playlist may indicate that a student will be engaged in small group collaboration for one period and individualized virtual instruction for another period—both activities focused on an identified math standard. The algorithm driving the playlist keeps building knowledge about the learner so it gets "smarter" about responding to individual needs. For example, cumulative information about the learner's past performance may alter the algorithm so it generates an alternative resource or strategy to present a challenging concept for a particular learner. The playlist keeps learners and teachers focused on needs and informed about progress.

The results of the School of One implementation are compelling. Thus, the concept is being scaled to more New York City middle schools and is being adopted by others via "Teach to One: Math," a non-profit entity initiated by key folks involved in the development of the School of One.

At the core of School of One is the commitment to base decisions about instruction on the needs of learners. Secondly, there is a willingness to implement a schedule which makes mathematics a priority in the school day. Tenets such as these provided a strong foundation for School of One. The School of One is a concrete example of how to make progress with the MCL vision. In fact, it may offer a potential starting point or next steps for other champions of customized teaching and learning.

○ Going Forward

Progress toward realizing the vision of MCL is made in steps. The explosion of attention on blended learning offers intriguing evidence of progress toward the vision. As a result, education stakeholders should watch its evolution and consider investing energies in the implementation of blended learning. We anticipate those experiences will serve you well in making substantial progress in the journey to make customized learning the rule, rather than the exception.

WEIGHT BEARING WALLS AS OPPORTUNITIES RATHER THAN BARRIERS

by James D. Parry

○ Connection to *inevitable*

Chuck and Bea's metaphor about weight bearing walls (WBWs) hits home with readers more than any topic in their book. Terms such as grades, grade levels, class periods, textbooks, and report cards conjure up familiar images. Memories—and emotions—come rushing back from one's school experiences. Via this metaphor, Chuck and Bea acknowledge the essential function of WBWs in schools. At the same time, they present compelling arguments for updating—actually replacing—WBWs with support structures which empower schools to respond to the needs of today's learners and incorporate 21st Century "building materials." Addressing the topic of WBWs deliberately and thoughtfully is a critical step in moving forward with the vision of MCL.

○ Primary Topic

Leadership, **Teaching and Learning**

○ Primary Audience

All stakeholders benefit from a shared understanding about the implications of WBWs.

○ Purpose

Thoughts about schools bring along thoughts about school structures, that is, WBWs. For nearly everyone, images of rows of desks, school bells, and report cards come to mind. While support structures are essential for today's schools, traditional WBWs contradict the vision of MCL. This resource engages stakeholders in a process for examining current WBWs with the intent of identifying opportunities and strategies for transitioning to more appropriate support structures for schools on the path of customized teaching and learning.

○ Rationale

While many education stakeholders recognize the constraints of traditional WBWs in schools, those structures are nearly sacred. In fact, it stretches many of us to picture schools without those "comfortable" images. And, the solution is not simply eliminating the familiar. Organizations need sound structures to ensure stability and support its work.

If we think in terms of remodeling a house, removing a weight bearing wall is possible. However, the contractor implements a system of heavy duty jacks as temporary supports until a new massive header bears the weight of the roof or upper floor. For education stakeholders, the hard thinking entails developing a plan for a desirable WBW replacement (a massive header) and implementing temporary supports (heavy duty jacks) as a transition to the advantageous result. It is a process. And the transition will be messy just as it is in a house remodeling project. Sort of a "no pain, no gain" process. Nonetheless, with a clear outcome in mind and a viable transition plan in place, the stress of the remodeling process is far outweighed by the gratifying changes which can benefit learners and enhance learning.

Despite the value and importance of addressing WBWs, the topic is nearly overwhelming and could easily become emotional for a group of stakeholders. Thus, stakeholders need a thoughtful and deliberate process which makes the topic of WBWs manageable and approachable.

○ Process for Use

This resource empowers school stakeholders to engage productively about the challenging yet critically important topic of WBWs. It offers a process focused on four outcomes:

1. Build shared understanding about the *real* and *perceived* barriers stemming from traditional WBWs as implemented in your school or district.
2. Identify a short list of possibilities by developing awareness of examples and strategies for shifting or pursuing alternatives to traditional WBWs.
3. Identify which WBW alternative presents the best opportunity for moving forward with the vision of MCL based on contextual factors about your school or district.
4. Develop a transition plan for implementing the alternative WBW.

Outcome #1: Build shared understanding about the *real* and *perceived* barriers stemming from traditional WBWs as implemented in your school or district.

In a recent discussion about ABC grades, I heard a school leader exclaim: "We must have grades or our students will not be accepted for college." On the surface, he stated a plausible argument given the common application process for colleges around the country. During the same discussion, a school counselor rebutted with: "In my work with college admission offices, I know that home-schooled students without letter grades achieve college entrance. Also, colleges accept international students who may not have grades to accompany their applications." Wow, a completely different lens on the same WBW of ABC grades!

The brief scenario about ABC grades reflects a classic dilemma associated with WBWs, that is, reality and perceptions about WBWs may be incongruent. It is a situation that warrants discussion by a group of stakeholders. In particular, the group should strive for a shared understanding about the *perceived* barriers associated with a specific WBW as compared to the *real* barriers. A discussion grounded with data and information equips group members with a lens for validating or refuting their respective perceptions and reaching a shared understanding.

The school leader in the scenario about ABC grades quickly noted his false perception. While still acknowledging the traditional path as the primary path to college entrance, he responded positively to the observation shared by the counselor. His change in thought did not minimize the challenge of pursuing a viable alternative to ABC grades. However, his shift in mindset no longer made thoughts of the current WBW insurmountable. As a result, he engaged with a new openness and energy for what might be possible.

A group of stakeholders may achieve Outcome #1 through a guided discussion of the list of the ten WBWs or a portion of that list as appropriate. (A list of ten WBWs is noted below as part of the process for Outcome #2.) A facilitator should focus the discussion using reflection questions such as:

- What are verifiable barriers to shifting a particular WBW?
- What are my perceptions of barriers associated with the WBW?
- How does increased awareness of the *real* and *perceived* barriers influence my thinking?
- What is our shared understanding of the barriers associated with the WBW?
- How does our shared understanding of barriers set the stage for viable opportunities to shift or replace WBWs?

Outcome #2: Identify a short list of possibilities by developing awareness of examples and strategies for shifting or pursuing alternatives to traditional WBWs.

While the group discussion accompanying Outcome #1 was essential, it emphasized barriers. Taking a negative approach to WBWs was not the intent. Gaining shared understanding about *real* barriers was the desired output of the group process. As a result, the stakeholders should be positioned to take on Outcome #2 with an emphasis on possibilities; that is, starting talk of productively shifting or replacing WBWs. However, the list of WBWs is plenty long; too many to tackle in one restructuring project even for the best of education stakeholders. Thus, the group needs a starting point, that is, a short list of ideas which energize folks and provide traction so that shifting and replacing WBWs becomes doable.

Toward that end, the following list of ten WBWs is shared. It contains a couple of starter ideas, examples, or strategies to stimulate discussion among a stakeholder group. The discussion of some WBWs may be brief as the group views it as too challenging or contentious for now. Other WBWs may merit a more lengthy discussion because the group views it as more approachable; perhaps viable as a relatively quick win that builds momentum. The group facilitator keeps the discussion moving yet focused on the outcome. The group attends to garnering a short list of ideas which holds potential and intrigues them. As a result, it is a "guided" brainstorming session; that is, it is bounded by bookends. One bookend is the stage set of Outcome #1 about barriers and the other bookend is the work of Outcome #3 when the stakeholder group will examine a few ideas through the filter of the context of their respective school. With that frame of reference, the stage is set for the list of WBWs with the discussion starting ideas.

1. **Grade Levels**
   - Shift to cross-grade or combined-grade classrooms.
   - Place learners in groups based on knowledge and skills rather than age.

2. **Students Assigned to Classrooms**
   - Structure day so all learners spend a portion of the day in a lab setting of individualized instruction and some portion in an assigned classroom of students.
   - Assign students to classrooms based on learner outcomes.

3. **Class Periods/Bell Schedule**
   - Implement a block schedule with variable times for length of blocks depending on learner outcomes.
   - Maintain a Monday-Wednesday-Friday schedule of more traditional class periods focused on content and initiate a Tuesday-Thursday schedule of extended periods focused on application and project-based experiences.

4. **Courses/Curriculum**
   - Shift to mastery of content or learner outcomes rather than credit for seat time.
   - Combine traditional subject matter classes and replace with cross-curricular experiences.

5. **Textbooks**
   - Redirect current resources for textbooks toward technology-based instructional materials.
   - Implement online textbooks for selected courses.

6. **Paper and Pencil**
   - Establish Google Docs or another online collaborative site as the primary "paper and pencil" for teachers and students.
   - Provide learners with a notebook computer, tablet computer, or handheld device as the primary alternative to "paper and pencil."

7. **ABC Grading System**
   - Replace letter grades for selected courses with rubrics which reflect and describe levels of competence for learning targets.
   - Maintain letter grades but improve grading practices such as eliminating "bonus points" and basing grades solely on evidence of demonstrating competence on learning targets.

8. **Report Cards**
   - Implement an electronic portfolio system which reflects and communicates the learner's competency.
   - Shift to a report card system that reflects progress on the achievement of learner outcomes.

9. **Learning Happens in School**
   - Encourage and give credit for online learning opportunities for students to gain knowledge and skills for achieving learning targets.
   - Establish partnerships with community entities for providing community-based, real-life learning opportunities.

10. **Nine Month School Year**
    - Implement a year-round school calendar with breaks scheduled throughout the year.
    - Develop a system of individualized summer learning plans for students which address specific learner outcomes.

Outcome #3: Identify which WBW alternative presents the best opportunity for moving forward with the vision of MCL based on contextual factors about your school or district.

With a short list of ideas in mind, the stakeholder group is positioned for a discussion about which is the best fit for their respective school or district. It is the process of translating the short list of possibilities produced via Outcome #2 to one or two defined possibilities that fit with the context of the respective school. The process for this outcome is driven by two key questions: **What** is the alternative WBW that is the best fit for our school? And, **why** are we pursuing that particular WBW?

Pursuing the **what** question requires discussion about contextual factors associated with the circumstances of your respective school or district. The context is the "story" or status of your school at this point in time. Starter questions to drive a discussion about context include:
- What are the highest instructional needs in our school given our student achievement data?
- Where do we have some momentum that we could build on or other initiatives with energy?
- Who are stakeholders (movers and shakers) in our school or district with the capacity and relationships essential for this challenging work?
- Who are potential partners in our community for helping us succeed with this work?
- What fiscal or other resources could we allocate toward this work?

The product of the discussion is shared understanding and clarity about contextual factors with an eye toward a logical fit or alignment with a proposed WBW.

Answering the **why** question is somewhat of a summative discussion for the group of stakeholders. They review the logical path they followed to reach an informed decision about the alternative WBW they choose to pursue. The group "connects the dots" between their goal of moving forward with the MCL vision and the proposed change of a WBW. As a result, from a big picture perspective, they know **why** they are pursuing the change—it moves them forward with their vision. From a pragmatic perspective, they can articulate **why** they are focused on this particular change—it is based on the realities and contexts of their respective school. Thus, the product of Outcome #3 is the identification of an alternative WBW which is grounded in a thoughtful, deliberate decision-making process.

Outcome #4: Develop a transition plan for implementing the alternative WBW.

Productive school leaders engage in action planning regularly as the tool for **how** to accomplish goals. Those skills are called for at this point in the process. The transition plan for implementing the alternative WBW should state a set of action steps, specify resources required, identify persons responsible, note time lines, and indicate benchmarks for formative assessment of progress. Once the plan is launched, the stakeholder group should meet periodically to review progress and make informed decisions about continuous improvement with the implementation as appropriate.

◉ Story

Recently at a rural K-12 district in a Midwestern town with the *inevitable* book study under their belt, I facilitated an energizing and productive discussion about WBWs. Designed as a variation of Outcomes #2 and #3, this process engaged small groups (4 to 6 elementary, middle school, or high school educators) with identifying the two WBWs they viewed as most approachable given their assessment of the context of the district. In the same regard, they were charged with noting which WBW was "untouchable" as they considered the district's context.

The dialogue was enlightening for group members as they wrestled with a wide range of observations and challenged one another about their thinking. As I listened in on conversations, I noted considerable consensus within the small groups. In part, their agreement stemmed from their common experience as groups of elementary, middle, or high school educators, respectively.

Each small group reported a synopsis of their discussion to the larger group underscoring the WBWs they identified as "approachable" and "untouchable." The large group dialogue which followed proved significantly more divergent than the small group discussions. For example, a couple of the elementary groups adamantly identified ABC Grading as the most approachable for change because of current successful efforts with non-graded report cards. Two high school groups were equally adamant that changing ABC Grading was on their untouchable list given parent attitudes and traditional college entrance requirements. Intrigued by the divergent views, participants listened attentively. As we wrapped up the activity, many voiced appreciation for the varied views and noted the value of the insights and group learnings which evolved—truly, a consensus building result for the group. They concluded with a commitment to build more shared understanding in coming weeks and indicated optimism about identifying the best possibilities for impacting WBWs constructively in their respective schools as well as across the district.

○ Going Forward

In working with education stakeholders, the topic of WBWs surfaces as the foremost obstacle. Despite the magnitude of the issue, stakeholders are eager to engage about potential alternatives to traditional WBWs and strategies to make such changes happen. As a result, the focus of those conversations shifts from constraints to possibilities! Their positive attitudes focused on possibilities encourage me in our efforts to confront the limitations of traditional WBWs.

As the education community addresses WBWs, I offer two observations. The first is that it is tough to change practices that are institutionalized over decades. How each school and team of stakeholders approaches the conundrum of WBWs depends in large part on contextual factors (Outcome #3). Some schools will be able to make major strides in relatively short time frames. That is my view of the efforts of the Carpe Diem Collegiate High School and Middle School. For valid reasons, other schools will experience progress with smaller steps over longer periods of time. For me, the pace of change is less important than the commitment to make progress with the vision of MCL.

My final observation in going forward: *Replace WBWs using a 21ˢᵗ Century approach.* I catch myself feeling relieved that I made a life adjustment to a reality of the Information Age only to discover that my adjustment needs to be followed by a new adjustment. Change and ongoing adaptations to change are characteristic of life in the 21ˢᵗ Century. I believe we need to apply that learning to our work with WBWs. Our thinking should be continuous improvement rather than institutionalizing new "walls." We need to embrace and respond thoughtfully and meaningfully to the potential and reality of the 21ˢᵗ Century.

ON THE ROAD TO A ROBUST TECHNOLOGY SYSTEM

by Julie Mathiesen

◎ Connection with *inevitable*

Customized learning is not about the technology, but technology is a key enabler. Chuck and Bea tell us that teaching is not a profession when it is conducted one to 25—that scenario is consistent with an industry focused on processing products in batches. Even the best, most accomplished teacher cannot provide customized learning each and every day for each and every child without the help of technology. In a technology-enabled learning environment we can capitalize on the best that technology has to offer for learning and we can capitalize on the human qualities that make a teacher an integral element of the learning environment.

◎ Primary Topic

Technology Resources

◎ Primary Audience

Technology leaders, superintendents and principals are the primary audience for this resource.

◎ Purpose

As we rebuild and restructure the current Weight Bearing Walls (WBWs) to bring schools out of the industrial age, we need robust technologies to play a supporting role. This resource presents a concrete description of technology components that are essential for a robust solution to support a customized learning system. The actual technologies will continue to change, evolve and improve, so there is no recommendation for a particular vendor or product. Transitioning to a customized learning system is more complex than purchasing a prescribed list of products from vendors X, Y and Z. Each learning system (school or district) will need to assess and determine where to leverage technology and acquire those technologies accordingly.

○ Rationale

If we eliminate the standard bell schedule and we don't assign students to particular classrooms or teachers, anarchy and chaos will ensue—*if* we don't have an alternate plan for organizing operations and tracking students. Once a student crosses the threshold into a school, the school then bears a responsibility for that student. Does the term *in loco parentis* ring a bell from your early educational studies? There is a very real and practical need for schools to know where students are and what they are doing. This is more than just a learning issue, it is a safety issue.

An MCL learning environment may include a variety of learning scenarios: face-to-face seminars, independent studies or work experiences in the community, completely autonomous online courses, small group discussions, project-based learning experiences, and blended classes where students move from more traditional teacher-driven sessions to more independent learning activities. How can we manage all these options? A robust technology system cannot only provide a <u>student</u> management system to manage a variety of student learning modalities, but it can also use that same data to bridge into a <u>learning</u> management system. The demographic information inherent to the student management system can help inform the needs of that student learner. For instance, if the student management system contains information about the preferred learning style and career interests of the student, that information feeds into the algorithm that helps *diagnose and prescribe* learning activities in the learning management system.

○ Process for Use

I suggest that you start by reviewing the recommended components of a customized technology system as described in this fieldbook resource. Then use your learnings from the review as a lens for assessing your current system. It may be as simple as adding a few more components or you may determine that you need a total revamp to move forward with MCL in your school. However, I suspect you have some of these components in place as most schools have at least a rudimentary student management system for attendance and basic logistical needs. In fact, many schools already incorporate aspects of the required infrastructure for a customized learning system. A fully realized customized learning system will merge, blend and synthesize all the needed components and associated data for the benefit of learners, learning coaches and school leaders.

○ The SIS

The foundation of the customized learning system rests on a robust student information system (SIS). This system is very logistical in nature and helps schools efficiently manage the role of *in loco parentis*. The system manages the student learner schedule; it lets students, parents, teachers and administrators know where everyone is supposed to be and when they are supposed to be there. It is appropriate for various stakeholders to have different levels of access and management. Each of the stakeholder groups would have a customized dashboard within the portal that allows them access to appropriate information for their respective roles and needs. Sophisticated systems will alert the appropriate stakeholder when a student is not in a designated location. The system has the ability to track absent and tardy students when physical attendance is important. Students and parents can track assignments and progress toward learning outcomes via an online portal to the system. Teachers can enter information about the status of learning objectives and these benchmarks can be fed into a report card-like feature at designated times.

Indeed the description provided for this SIS does not sound groundbreaking or innovative—in fact, it probably sounds much like a system your school already uses. An SIS that supports customized learning must have additional features that support a customized learning schedule. For example, if a student chooses a "Building and Defending a Business Plan" seminar for a two week period, enrolls in an online self-paced study of Algebra Concepts, engages in a work-study experience on Monday mornings with a local architect, meets with a project-based learning team on Monday, Wednesday and Fridays at 4:00 PM, participates in a weekly and variable planning/update session with her learning coach and attends track practice at 7:00 AM five days a week--things quickly get complicated! A robust system must facilitate this level of complexity in a fluid and dynamic manner which addresses needs associated with the teaching and learning process for learners as well as needs associated with the managing and documenting process for school personnel.

First thoughts might prompt the reaction that a mass of complex student schedules would be too chaotic and impossible to manage. However, it's very possible and completely sensible that some chunks of the schedule would be consistent and stable throughout the school term. For instance, seminars could be pre-scheduled throughout the year and students would then have flexibility to schedule them to fit with other learning activities. Or to a large degree, the slate of online courses that are available could be predefined. By using the technology of an SIS to increase our efficiency, we can manage what might first look like chaos. We can do a great deal of planning and organization based on what we know about student learning needs while still accommodating personal choice and customization.

The SIS should also house valuable demographic data about students; data that help us *diagnose and prescribe* the best learning scenarios for the needs of students. For instance, I'm aware of schools that utilize stand-alone software programs to help students learn about careers. Typically this type of program engages students with inventories about interests and learning styles. This is incredibly valuable information that typically is never integrated into a larger, comprehensive system to support and make informed decisions about student learning. A company called Appleton Learning provides test preparation and academic coaching for students. The first step in their process is gathering data to determine the "Genius Style" of learners for purposes of matching coaches with learners. This example reflects the type of data that should be incorporated into the SIS to make it more comprehensive and responsive to learner needs.

The LMS

The SIS must be tightly integrated with a Learning Management System (LMS). Typically, this is a separate technology silo that never *talks* to the SIS. In a customized learning environment, we use what we know about the student to make decisions about the best learning path for each student. A really great teacher can do this to some degree with a small group of learners, but it is a huge challenge to do it all day, every day. Educators need the assistance of technology to make this process efficient. Equally important, the technology makes it accessible—both to the teacher and the learner. This aspect of the system is critical if students are to be active players in their own learning experience.

As the residence for the curriculum content, the LMS allows for customized materials, structures and processes to support day-to-day learning experiences. The LMS can take the place of everything students carry in backpacks or shove into lockers. A 30 pound stack of textbooks might be replaced by open, free and fee online resources widely available. That is, resources that are more engaging, that adjust for different readiness/achievement levels, that accommodate personal learning styles and that are accessed via subject matter of interest to the learner.

Like the SIS, you are probably familiar with a variety of LMS systems. There are a handful of large commercial products that are well known in the K-12 and higher education markets. Recently, there has been a wave of more open source tools and products making their way to the mainstream. Justifiably, some open sources have taken a bad rap primarily because they automated traditional practices of a single track for slogging through mind-numbing content. Additionally, graphical interfaces for early LMS were less than friendly—neither teachers nor learners could figure out how to maximize the potential of the tool.

An LMS that facilitates customized learning will support a different kind of teacher-student relationship. From *inevitable*, we know that a customized learning environment supports more learner autonomy and more control of the learning experience. One of the functions of the LMS will be to deliver a customized playlist of learning objects for the learner. Essentially, the playlist is a learner-centered lesson plan. Both the learner and learning coach will have the opportunity to edit this playlist, based on what the learning coach knows about the learner's needs as well as what the learner knows about his own needs. The two parties will have the ability to mediate the progression of learning. This progression or playlist contains a wide variety of learning objects. Some of the learning objects may be very traditional, a chapter from an online textbook or a graphic organizer that help make meaning of a complex subject. Other learning objects may come in the form of text or video to help the learner work with others to plan a project-based learning experience.

One of the most common sources of learning objects will be resources from the internet. An especially promising project that demonstrates the notion of playlists and learning objects can be found at www. goorulearning.org. The developers are committed to honoring the human right to education and have made all resources free to students across the world. Learners and learning coaches can access individual resources or they can access resources that have already been structured as a playlist; Gooru calls these collections. Gooru is in beta form at the time of this writing, so structures and the vocabulary of those structures may change; however, it gives educators a good sense of emerging online products addressing curriculum and content needs.

The Recommendation Engine

A big part of my role in sharing the story of customized learning is speaking at events across the country to build awareness. One of the pop culture examples I use to help make the idea of a recommendation engine for education more tangible is Amazon. In fact, I refer to it a bit flippantly as—the Amazon "magic." Amazon uses complex algorithms to help predict what I may want to buy. Their "magic" saves me from browsing one million books to find something in a genre I prefer—also, it is a win for Amazon because I buy more books (ebooks, of course).

Notably, the programming that supports this "magic" is accessible for education and it is morally imperative that we employ it to customize learning for today's students. A sophisticated recommendation engine can search across the sea of learning objects that live on the internet—frequently referred to as "the cloud." In reality, information lives on the ground in servers, but the accessibility of the internet makes it feel like we can pull it out of thin air. In addition to looking across sites like Gooru to curate learning objects, the recommendation engine will also search millions of other learning resources that exist online or in the cloud. It may use metadata from the Learning Registry, an online resource for digital curriculum, to match learning objects that are associated with specific standards or other identified learning outcomes. Increasingly more and more of these learning objects are available for free and are commonly called "open educational resources" or OER. The recommendation engine will *pull* appropriate learning objects from providers such as Thinkfinity, Gooru, iTunesU, CK-12 and LearnZillion. School leaders could also collaborate with selected vendors to feed fee-based products into the recommendation engine. Perhaps schools would even want to employ teacher-designers to create more learning objects. The possibilities are vast.

The recommendation engine will serve as the interface to the rest of the world and all it has to offer and contribute to the pursuit of a customized teaching and learning process. The engine will generate playlists of learning objects that are content specific, student specific, learning style specific, interest specific, and achievement level specific. The LMS will deliver this playlist to be mediated by the learning coach and the student learner on a daily basis.

Story

As an advocate of progressive education and because I have a tendency to be a bit of a "helicopter mom" (Google it), I pushed for my middle school child to take an online course as part of his regular school day. Since this was a new experience for someone enrolled at his school, I appreciated the administrative support I received for my son to try this option. I thought it was very important that he engage in this type of learning experience to prepare him for future learning opportunities.

When it came time to actually schedule this course, we bumped up against the school's student management system. The administrative support staff person was quite puzzled about how this new type of learning opportunity could possibly work with the current management system. In an attempt to help solve her dilemma, I suggested scheduling his class during the first or last hour of the school day so he could just stay home to take his online course. Her response: "But then who would take his attendance, and how would we make him fit into the system?" Although the people of the school supported this variation, the rigid technology system only allowed an on-campus schedule with a student present for all class periods. The resolution was to trick the system into thinking my son was "somewhere" and the school librarian had to take responsibility for managing his attendance for the designated hour. Clearly, the system was designed for administrative convenience rather than meeting learner needs.

I am optimistic that a comprehensive, customized learning system will not only accommodate the small variation we sought for my son's middle school experience, it will also accommodate the ever changing needs of learners.

○ Going Forward

The parts and pieces of a comprehensive customized learning system already exist—but we've yet to see them all working synchronously to support a truly customized learning environment. But be encouraged because several systems are being piloted with compelling results. For example, take note of the School of One described in the fieldbook resource titled *Schools On the Move with Customization*. Learners and educators at that school already are experiencing the value and benefit of a playlist for guiding the teaching and learning experience of mathematics for middle school students. While we wait for refinement and scalability of such tools for the mass market, we can build our experience with currently available infrastructure components. That will position us for ramping in to a comprehensive system for customizing teaching and learning.

BALANCING ACT: THEORETICAL AND PRACTICAL

by Patricia Peel

Connection to *inevitable*

As leaders, we constantly engage in a balancing act between the theoretical and the practical, particularly when technology is foundational to applying the theory under discussion. When you picture mass customized learning (MCL), does a balancing act come to mind? How will you cultivate the theoretical possibilities of doing school differently while answering the "yeah, but" practical technology questions of the teacher down the hall? They might sound something like this: "How do you expect me to do customized learning with 125 ninth grade English students when I share one laptop lab with six other department members? Oh, and I can't count on the wireless network working." How do you think your staff will greet the dismantling of the weight bearing walls discussed in Chapter 8 if they do not have access to functional technology hardware and a reliable, stable and secure network?

Primary Topic

Leadership, Technology Resources

Primary Audience

This resource is intended for individuals providing leadership oversight for the technology foundational to planning, implementing, and sustaining customized teaching and learning. Those individuals might include the superintendent, instructional leader, principal, and technology leader.

Purpose

Leaders balance the theoretical, which is the customized teaching and learning vision, with the practical, which is technology-related: Where are my computers? Is the network operating? How am I supposed to customize learning anyway? These are legitimate, day-to-day, application-level concerns related to hardware and network access along with technical support availability and teacher capacity to facilitate students learning differently.

The purpose of this article is to help with your technology "yeah, buts." By conducting an audit of the district's equipment, staffing and process, professional development, and enterprise management you can address burning questions. Data gathered can support you with long term, big picture aspects of a shift to customized learning as well as provide direction for short term goals aimed at building a solid foundation on which to erect new structures to replace the current weight bearing walls. In the process, you will build trust and credibility with your staff as you respond, directly and transparently, to their burning questions about how to operationalize the customized learning vision. In other words, you will have hard data to address the "yeah buts" so that MCL is not DOA.

Rationale

You may be thinking: "How does this help me with the 'yeah, buts...?' Enough audits already!" If so, this might be the perfect moment to hit the pause button, take a deep breath, and recall Chuck and Bea's Total Leadership discussion in Chapter 10. They describe Strategic Design as branching into *Strategic Direction* and *Strategic Alignment*. In the long run *(Strategic Direction)*, a systems audit helps frame a meta-level picture. In the short run *(Strategic Alignment)*, specific technology and infrastructure audits provide micro-level snapshots of the environment in which the teacher down the hall and her department members work each day with students. These can be powerful data with which to answer burning questions and to create a sense of urgency for needed change. You might consider the use of the technology audit as an entry ramp to the customized learning highway. Once you have clear direction, you can thoughtfully and deliberately plan your journey for increasing the use of technology as a tool in student learning. Going that distance in the short run moves you down the highway toward achieving the long-term vision of customized learning.

In addition, the audit tool provides a framework and language that readily translate into an action plan as you consider next steps in your overall *Strategic Design*. As indicated in the fieldbook resource, *Facing Reality: An Audit,* an audit can be repeated and reported on as we evaluate whether or not the work reaps a valid return on investment, moving us forward to our "preferred future for our learners."

Process For Use

Getting started:

1. **Why** – First establish the need for an audit. Gather background information (including historical) that paints the picture of your current context. Frame key questions that the school/district needs to have answered; this provides a rationale for the process and will be a data source. For example, these key questions can be consistently used with different focus groups to provide targeted feedback. Another powerful use for the over-arching questions comes into play as the process unfolds and tensions and/or conflicts arise. The questions can be used to remind individuals of the purpose of the survey and what the data can ultimately assist the school or district in accomplishing. In other words, the data-gathering stage leads to a broader decision-making process that will ultimately

answer key questions based on your own data as well as research and industry-based recommendations.

2. **Who** – Identify audit leadership. Once designated, this team will determine if the audit will be conducted by internal staff or, depending on resources and need, by an outside consultant/team. In some instances, having an objective "critical friend" gather the data and report to key constituents is advantageous. The leadership team (and consultant if applicable) will identify key individuals and/or focus groups to be interviewed. Consider including representatives from administration, teachers, students, technology department and/or technical support. Designate either a school or district designee or a consultant responsible for gathering input needed to score and report the individual strategy efficiency levels.

3. **What** – To conduct an audit, you will need a tool or an instrument to assess the efficiency levels in the areas you have identified. As you develop your own tool customized to assess local needs, you may find the ***Technology Support Index (TSI)***[1] a helpful resource to support your work.

4. **Where** – The audit can be conducted at either the school or district level.

5. **When** – The leadership team will craft a timeline in context of internal benchmark dates that might include consideration for the following: budget cycles, board meeting schedules, regularly scheduled meetings, or in-service dates. In addition, particular circumstances might indicate the need to compress the timeline or might allow for a more deliberate process. A comprehensive timeline will include all pertinent activities from the initial planning sessions through a variety of reporting forums including a presentation to your local school board.

◎ Story

"Yeah, but…..this is how we've always done it!" That statement is rarely made without some strong feelings attached. I certainly heard it as a central office leader in two different districts, which grappled with similar technology-related issues. In each case, we contracted with Technology and Innovation in Education (TIE), who used the ***TSI***[1] as the audit (data-gathering) tool. The process and tool provided a comprehensive picture of district-wide technology by supplying data to help us frame answers to key questions.

Why an outside contractor? In partnership with district leadership, they bring a particular skill set to the project and may represent an objective, expert voice at the table when presenting data and information to different audiences. In both districts, having a consultant assist with gathering the data, summarizing the data, and presenting the data clearly communicated the importance attached to the project and our intent to "get it right." Along the way, our TIE partners were excellent resources and "critical friends" assisting the less-techie with building background knowledge and providing industry-based information. They supported our balancing act as we dealt with the practical in order to implement the theoretical.

Lessons learned? A wise person once said, "You may argue with me, but you can't argue with your own data." Another sage echoed, "Process, process, process." Facilitating a well thought out, respectful process that highlights organizational data along with research and industry-based recommendations can promote the use of technology as a tool to accelerate student learning. In the short run, a foundation for new weight bearing walls needed to support customized learning is laid. In the long run, the teacher down the hall is able to focus on student learning because the weight bearing walls are transparent. The "yeah, buts…." are DOA; the MLC vision is alive and well.

○ Going Forward

The *TSI*[1], which is referenced in the **Process for Use** section of this resource, was developed by Dr. Chip Kimball in conjunction with the International Society for Technology in Education (ISTE) and the Gates Foundation. While perhaps dated in some regards, the tool remains an excellent resource for schools and districts to consider as they prepare a survey to profile technology support programs and provide solutions based on those unique profiles.

Several pieces of the *TSI*[1] legacy are worth modeling as you craft a customized, local technology survey instrument. Consider retaining these two *TSI*[1] assumptions: (1) current network infrastructure is either in place or is planned for each classroom and (2) all four domains of support are required.

The four domains indicated below remain current and applicable:
- **Equipment Standards** – Focuses on consistent equipment and software decisions that can directly impact the quality of support provided.
- **Staffing and Processes** – Addresses technical assistance staffing and the support practices used that can impact efficiencies in support.
- **Professional Development** – Considers how strong professional development can change the nature of organizational support requirements and impact a team's ability to provide support.
- **Enterprise Management** – Identifies strategies that capitalize upon the technology itself to provide strong support.

While some *TSI*[1] indicators supporting the four domains are current, others could be added or edited as appropriate. For example, under Enterprise Management, the current topic of provisions for students to bring their own device (byod) is not addressed.

Modeling that data will indicate the school's or district's ability to address each strategy in terms of efficiency levels and also predict the accompanying fiscal implications ranging from neutral to significant, remains helpful for your future planning needs.

○ References

[1] *Technology Support Index (Version 2.0)*: http://www.p12.nysed.gov/technology/resources /TechnologySupportIndex_v2.0.pdf.

GETTING READY FOR ROLLOUT: TECHNOLOGY ASSUMPTION

by Patricia Peel

○ Connection to *inevitable*

In Chapter 10, Chuck and Bea "apply the Total Leaders Framework to the planning for, and the implementation of mass customized learning" (MCL). They note that when promoting new visions, you must "run well ahead of your present capacity to implement them." This should not prevent you from dreaming. Instead, our author friends suggest that you need to be ready to "paint a concrete picture of change." Chuck and Bea help us prepare with their list of seven critical elements needed for rollout. As a leader poised to promote the customized learning vision, referencing the rollout list can guide and assist you with refining your thinking as you "begin with the end in mind."[1]

A step to refining that thinking should include a close examination of the "ready for rollout" list and particular attention to Chuck and Bea's caution that "all is in place" including "that systems have been tested." In that context, a review of rollout steps two through seven reveals an inherent *technology assumption*. Although not stated explicitly, successful implementation implicitly requires a fully functional technology system. Knowing what you need in advance of implementation helps you strategically paint the picture of change—a picture that includes rollout-ready technology.

○ Primary Topic

Leadership, Technology Resources

○ Primary Audience

The primary audience includes individuals in key leadership roles who are responsible for technology leadership and implementation at the district and building levels including: superintendent, school board members, instructional leaders, technology leaders, technology support staff, staff developers, and principals.

○ Purpose

Have you ever been poised to launch a systemic change or initiative only to have an underlying assumption questioned at the last minute, which caused you to delay the launch and go back to the drawing board? Worse, have you had the misfortune of launching an initiative only to have a foundational piece called into question? In other words, you were out there in public, "painting the picture of change," and someone kicked over your paint can! The purpose of this resource is to make explicit technology-related topics that you need to consider when a rollout of customized learning is your "end in mind."

○ Rationale

In Chapter 2, Chuck and Bea discuss "new whiz-bang technologies" that have and will continue to transform how we do things in our everyday lives. They advocate that these same technologies have the ability to transform how students learn. The underlying assumption is these technologies are readily available, are supported, and that staff and learners are proficient consumers. Testing the underlying assumption early in the customized teaching and learning exploration process can arm you with powerful data and information as you prime the canvas for the MCL painting.

○ Process for Use

The table below, based on my work in a mid-western school district, includes technology-related topics impacting our ability to meet the district mission. In tandem with a District Strategic Planning process initiated by the superintendent, we considered the technology area as a related systemic piece critical to "Prepare all students to meet the challenges of an ever-changing world."

As you review the list below, you may identify areas of strength. You may also identify an area or areas that are in need of attention, that are not in the "assumed ready for seamless use" category. Use the list as it suits your purposes as a ramping in point.

Use with caution: If your review of this list indicates areas of need, do not become discouraged about the possibilities of customized learning! I repeat, do not throw up your hands in defeat. Rather, celebrate that you have a clearer picture of what needs attention so that you can strategically move technology into the assumption category. Paint the picture of change for staff, learners, and community by outlining your processes to remove roadblocks (i.e.: identified technology weaknesses); you will win advocates and silence naysayers.

Technology Assumption	Considerations
Multi-year Technology Plan	• Consider a three (3) year plan that provides future direction but is a short term enough to provide high flexibility. Your state or district may already have a prescribed template to follow. If not, the ISTE *Technology Support Index (TSI)*[2] may provide guidance. • You can develop an annual action plan based on the multi-year plan proposed above. The action plan, including a timeline, can guide your planning, follow -up and project assessment.
Enterprise System	• The network chunk may include the following: cloud-based management services, onsite servers, authentication protocols, security, server network monitoring software and hardware, data backup system, and provisions for a "safe" server room environment. The goal is to provide a highly reliable, secure, and maintainable network. • Consider that connectivity includes both wired and wireless access as hardware use increases. You might also consider making provisions for a student to "bring your own device" (byod). • Email and other basic operating systems need to be centrally distributed and administered.
Equipment/Hardware	• Technology as a tool includes but is not limited to: desktops, laptops, tablet devices, and handhelds for student and adult learners. • Consider that an interactive presentation system per classroom can be a means to stretch limited resources and actively engage students in learning. • You may consider planning and implementing a hardware "rotation cycle" that becomes an effective tool for budgeting, purchasing and inventory purposes.
Tech Support	• Adequate department-wide technology staffing that supports the infrastructure and tech support is essential. "Staffing" could include students earning wages or credit, including an internship or logging volunteer hours, for project-based learning. • Identify a tech support delivery model. A Help Desk Model is one example.

Job Descriptions	• A review of current job descriptions outlining all tech-related jobs could include: management, infrastructure, tech support, data processing and mining, web page development and maintenance, tech-related professional development, and student workers/aides/interns. Depending on your organization, supporting staff development positions, such as integrationist, may also be appropriate.
Professional Development (PD)	• PD is needed for the tech staff, instructional and support staff. Within the tech department, cross training may be necessary along with opportunities to keep skills and certifications current. • Tech staff may be responsible for providing training to instructional and support staff on technical topics while integrationists or instructional staff developers may provide support on using technology as a tool for instruction. Considering who best supports particular skills (basic tech skills versus instruction) is a means to maximize limited resources, both fiscal and staffing.
Policy	• A policy review to cross-reference federal, state and local compliance along with addressing any customized learning-related issues is warranted. Common tech-related policy topics include: electronic network and technology use; network and computer systems; inclusion of the Children's Internet Protection Act, proper use, educational use, disciplinary (student and staff) and ethical behavior.
Communication Tools	• Webpages are the "front doors' by which your public accesses the district, school, and teachers. Along with evaluating visual appeal, navigation ease is a priority for maximizing a customized learning web page presence. • Customized learning requires transparent parent/student/teacher communication. Consider how your web page and other systems support that capability. • Collaborative tools, such as wikis, need to be available for school or classroom-level learning communities. How these will be made available is both a logistics and policy decision.
Data Mining	• The need for mining data will grow exponentially as you move into customized learning. Anticipating the compatibility between software and programs to support instruction, assessment, grading and other will pay dividends. For example, on-line assessment data is useless to teachers and students unless readily available.

○ Story

Most of us are familiar with the phrase "a perfect storm." It is an expression that describes an event where a rare combination of circumstances will aggravate a situation drastically, which can result in an event of unusual magnitude. But perfect storms do not just occur in nature. A perfect storm can converge in a district or school when circumstances align.

This seemed to be the case in the district where I was assistant superintendent responsible for curriculum, instruction, and technology. We had a number of initiatives in play or topics under discussion including the following:

- District strategic planning discussion highlighted the need to promote 21st Century Skills prompting a wide range of discussions including professional development.
- Extensive K-12 curriculum work triggered hardware availability questions including classroom computers, school-level labs, and classroom presentation systems.
- District-wide Assessment Plan development prompted an on-line assessment discussion (and pending decision).
- Data-mining and report-writing needs across the district increased significantly.
- Technology-delivered curriculum purchases were escalating.
- The high school engaged in a process to explore the possibilities of a 1:1 initiative. This prompted discussions ranging from policies, to hardware, to infrastructure, to tech support and professional development.
- As a result of strategic planning and the 1:1 discussion, the recommendation to re-evaluate our district, school and teacher web pages was brought forward.
- Aging district-wide network hardware and accompanying software reached a critical juncture.
- Wireless access inconsistencies were increasingly reported.
- In context of the items above, the ability to deliver pro-active tech support had decreased dramatically; department staffing levels were in question.

Viewed separately, the items above are projects or topics on any school's or district's "to do" list. Things that need attention or that may be next in line for budget consideration. Viewed collectively, the list creates a sense of urgency to take decisive steps. The *Technology Assumption/Consideration* table highlights the key areas that ultimately needed attention in order to avert the 'perfect storm' brewing on the horizon.

In the case of the district under discussion, the perfect storm never hit. Leadership explicitly addressed each of the key areas. As a result, it is currently well-positioned with technologies that are readily available, are supported, and the staff and learners are proficient technology consumers.

◎ Going Forward

Outstanding national, regional, state and/or local resources are available as you explore each of the "ready for roll out" areas identified in the *Technology Assumption/Consideration* table. Sources may include the following: consultants, on-line resources, professional contacts, compliance guidelines, and the collective wisdom gleaned as various groups process your particular topics or issues. Once the technology assumption is clearly addressed, you have a ramp-on point to "paint the concrete picture of change" for customized teaching and learning.

◎ References

[1]Covey, Stephen R. (1989). *The seven habits of highly effective people: Powerful lessons in personal change.* New York: Free Press.

[2] *Technology Support Index (Version 2.0)* http://wwwp12.nysed.gov/technology/resources/TechnologySupportIndex_v2.0pdf.

MINIMIZING THE RISK;
MAXIMIZING THE DECISION

by Nancy Hall

○ Connection with *inevitable*

The Epilogue chapter in **inevitable** asks the question, "What's in it for you?" Why would you want to begin down the path of customized teaching and learning? You really do need to answer that question! As Chuck and Bea so honestly point out, "We are asking for a massive, systemic, transformational change. A change of this scope, in a very mature profession, is difficult to initiate, to implement, and to sustain. It takes authentic and courageous leadership." I would add that it takes risk, but there are ways to minimize your risk and maximize your chances for success if you carefully consider the decision to customize teaching and learning prior to starting the initiative.

○ Primary Topic

Leadership, Human Resources

○ Primary Audience

For a superintendent with a "one career shot," the risk in proposing to the school board to transform the local educational system may seem too high. However, the superintendents that I know would also be professionally torn by being too cautious and preventing the board from seeing customized teaching and learning as the best opportunity for 21st Century learners. How can the decision to begin this journey be made less risky and more successful for superintendents, school boards, principals, teachers, parents, and learners?

○ Purpose

Uncertainty about the future causes the risk in our decisions. We need to act now, but we don't know for certain what will happen until it happens. We have to be able to make quality assessments about the future. We know our assessments can be biased, ill-informed, or poorly thought through. The challenge is to make assessments for our most strategic decisions that truly reflect what our most informed people believe and what we all believe is best for learners. The purpose of this resource is to reach alignment with stakeholders on the quality of the decision to implement customized teaching and learning before the decision is made.

◎ Rationale

I had the good fortune to learn about risk-taking and decision-making from Leo Hopf[1]. Leo is founder and CEO of Teamhopf. He works as a consultant to guide international corporations in their strategic decisions. He teaches at Stanford University and Carlson School of Management at the University of Minnesota. In 2010, he co-authored an award-winning book titled ***Rethink, Reinvent, and Reposition***. He has given me permission to share his risk-taking and decision-making tool with you and apply it to this courageous educational decision.

In the seminars that I attended with Hopf, I learned that the quality of a decision is limited by the weakest point in the decision-making process. Using the customized teaching and learning decision as an example:

What if you had done a great job on everything else, but your depth of knowledge about customized teaching and learning was poor? Garbage in, garbage out.

What if you had done a great job on everything else, but customized teaching and learning really didn't fit with your district's mission, vision, core values, and beliefs? You solved the wrong problem.

What if you had done a great job on everything else, but your analysis of the execution phase was poor? You get the right answer, but no one cares. Nothing ever happens.

The tool in this resource will take you through Hopf's decision-making process which can guide you as to whether your district is ready for this decision, and it will position your implementation efforts for the greatest chance of success.

◎ Process for Use

1) Hopf uses a simple scale to judge the readiness for decision-making and managing risk—the traffic light.

Red means stop. There is not yet sufficient understanding to make a quality decision. At this stage you probably do not know the correct questions to ask.

Yellow means proceed with caution. Making a decision now is risky as there is much yet to do. Most of the right questions are known, but not the answers.

Green means go. You have done sufficient work to make the decision. More work to refine will not be worth the additional time and effort. You have credible answers to most of the key questions.

2) Hopf has identified seven decision-making attributes that need to be carefully examined and rated red, yellow, or green by the group of stakeholders you assemble. Those attributes include examining your structure, alternative choices, knowledge, objectives, evaluation of risk and return, determining the capacity for a quality execution of the decision, and considering the attributes of the people and the culture in your district.

Structure: What is the context for this decision? Is it consistent with our vision, mission, and core values? Is this the right scope of change for our organization? How does it compare to other opportunities?

Choices: Are there more choices? Do these choices span the range?

Knowledge: Says who? Based upon what? What if they are wrong?

Objectives: Can we afford the loss? Are there important non-financial attributes?

Evaluation: Are the assumptions wise? Do the results make sense? How sensitive is the result to changes in the inputs from our people?

Execution: Will we really stick it out? Do we have the skills, systems, and resources needed to "win?"

People, culture: What aspects of our culture will help us and which aspects will hurt us in implementation? What is our attitude toward risk?

3) Specific questions enable the stakeholders to rate the district on each attribute. Those questions are attached to this resource as a tool.

4) The stakeholders work hard to move ratings of reds to yellows and yellows to greens through the use of their specific action plans, gathering information, and talking to others within the district in between meetings.

In a series of about four meetings over a period of two months, the stakeholders' task is to focus their decision-making conversations on moving the ratings of red to yellows and the ratings of yellows to greens. The group can visually keep track of their progress in a chart like the one below. All attributes do not need to be in the green scale in order for a quality decision to be made. For example, in the chart below a quality decision could have been made after meeting number three. If after several meetings many attributes are still in the red and yellow range, the initiative to implement customized teaching and learning at this time would be deemed a high risk. In the Going Forward section of this resource there are further suggestions regarding how you can reduce your risk and reconsider this decision at another time.

	Meeting 1	Meeting 2	Meeting 3	Meeting 4
Objectives	yellow	green	green	green
Structuring	green	green	green	green
Choices	red	yellow	green	green
Knowledge	red	yellow	yellow	green
Evaluation	red	red	yellow	green
Execution	red	yellow	green	green
People & Culture	green	green	green	green

◎ Story

After attending a seminar by Hopf at the University of Minnesota, I contracted with him to conduct a similar seminar at my educational institution. We were facing serious financial difficulty and our leadership team knew we needed to take some risks to meet that challenge while continuing to grow and develop as an institution. Hopf facilitated a fun simulation with us about risk-taking. He asked for a volunteer from the audience who would invest $20 in a venture with him. The success of the venture would be determined by the toss of a coin. "Heads" would leverage that investment into $60 (for real!) and "tails" would lose the total $20 investment.

The administrator sitting next to me took Hopf's challenge and handed over a $20 bill. Then Hopf asked this administrator how much additional money he would pay for "perfect information" before the coin was tossed and the call was made. After some deliberation, this administrator decided not to pay for additional information. Then Hopf asked if the administrator would like to take on a partner to invest with him and reimburse $10 of the original investment so his potential loss would only be $10 instead of $20. Of course his potential winnings would be cut in half as well to $30. The administrator liked this idea, and I agreed to be the partner investor. The coin toss took place and we won $60 from Hopf!

What I learned from this simulation is that educators don't have to take on risks alone. In fact, they can reduce their risk by purchasing information, resources, and talent that might make the difference in achieving success. They can take also take on partners to add resources and minimize losses. CESA1, a cooperative educational agency serving 45 school districts in southeastern Wisconsin, is a prime example of an organization that used such a risk-minimizing strategy to implement personalized learning. They partnered with the Wisconsin Department of Public Instruction and the Council of Chief State School Officers to add resources and gain public support. Read on for more details.

⊙ Going Forward

CESA1 published a paper in May 2011 entitled "Public Education Transformation Powered by Regional Networks." The document can be found on their website at www.cesa1.k12.wi.us . In the opening remarks, the author of this paper states: "Community members often react to change with skepticism or distrust. In addition, friction between key stakeholders, including teachers, administrators, school boards, parents and the community at-large, can impede progress. Being a transformation leader can be a challenging position for an individual district to be in, but the mantle of multiple school district involvement offers the opportunity for greater benefits and progress with less risk."

The CESA1 cooperative staff assists superintendents in the participating districts to:
- Increase awareness and understanding of the need for public education transformation
- Facilitate the exchange of information among organizations and individuals interested in public education transformation through networking opportunities and technology
- Secure and align resources to support regional public education transformation efforts
- Provide consulting services and professional development opportunities
- Promote student, teacher, parent and community engagement
- Advocate for policy that enables transformation

The Wisconsin Department of Public Instruction supported the CESA #1 transformation efforts through the designation of CESA #1 as an "Innovation Zone," which allowed the necessary conditions for innovation to take place in the participating districts.

The Council of Chief State School Officers selected CESA #1 Wisconsin to participate in the Partnership for Next Generation Learning (NxGL) Innovation Lab Network, a national effort sponsored by the Stupski Foundation and the Council of Chief State School Officers to "design, develop and test practices, strategies and structures that hold the potential to transform learning." As the NxGL Innovation Lab Network has evolved, Wisconsin has now connected with five other states to provide access to additional individuals and organizations interested in the Personalized Learning Initiative.

Way to go, Wisconsin, in minimizing risk and maximizing the personalized learning decision!

⊙ Reference

[1]Hopf, L., & Welter, W. (2011). *Rethink, reinvent, and reposition: 12 strategies to renew your business and boost your bottom line.* Avon, MS: Adams Business.

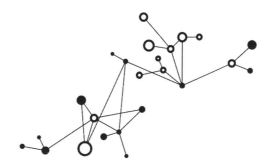

MINIMIZING THE RISK; MAXIMIZING THE DECISION TOOL

Adapted by Nancy Hall with permission from Leo Hopf

◎ Structuring

Where does the decision to implement customized teaching and learning fit within our school district's priorities? How could this decision further our district's goals? How does this decision align with our vision, mission, core values, and strategic plan? Which of our student outcomes would be strengthened by this effort? What are the key challenges? Who will lead this effort and what percentage of their time will be spent on this effort? Who else will be involved? Is the project schedule clear in terms of deliverables and responsibilities?

How would we rate the readiness of our structure for making this decision?

Red _____ Yellow _____ Green _____

What specific action can we take to answer important questions about structuring?

◎ Choices

How attractive is this opportunity? How large are the barriers to success? Are there state and national trends making this opportunity to customize teaching and learning more or less attractive? What gaps do we have for successful execution? How large are they, and how difficult will it be to fill them? What must we do ourselves and what can be outsourced? What other agencies could become partners in implementation?

How would we rate our examination of choices?

Red _____ Yellow _____ Green _____

What specific action can we take to improve choices? _____

⊙ Knowledge

What do we know well and what is less clear to us regarding customized teaching and learning? Who will provide the information for each uncertainty? Are these people credible to the board? Do we have other comparable districts that could serve as models? Do we clearly understand the critical issues throughout the opportunity? Do we have a real understanding of how customized learning will meet learner needs and impact teachers? How would we rate our knowledge?

Red _____ Yellow _____ Green _____

What specific action can we take to improve our knowledge? _____

⊙ Objectives

Which groups have a major stake in the decision to implement customized teaching and learning? What does each of these groups want and how would they prioritize what they want through this implementation? How confident are we that we really understand these wants and priorities? How can we refine our decision to address the desires of the different groups? What trades can be made that place the highest importance on the decisions with the most benefit for student learning?

How would we rate where we are in understanding the objectives of the major stakeholder groups?

Red _____ Yellow _____ Green _____

What specific action can we take to improve our understanding of stakeholder objectives?

_____

⊙ Evaluation

Which uncertainties have the largest effect on the overall value of the initiative? What can we do to improve our understanding of the key uncertainties? What is the risk and return of this initiative? What is our gut feeling? Can we explain the main insights to the public in layman's terms? What can we do to increase the upside of this initiative and to limit its downside? How would we rate our understanding of key uncertainties?

Red _____ Yellow _____ Green _____

What specific action can we take to decrease risk? _____

◎ Execution

Does everyone who needs to say yes to this initiative agree? Is it clear to what they are agreeing? Are the implications spelled out? Does everyone understand the magnitude of the value of a successful execution and the reduction in value a poor execution would cause? Is there a communication plan which addresses the needs of key stakeholders? What actions need to happen to ensure successful implementation? By when should they happen? What resources will be required and by when? How is this decision tied to the budgeting process? What must change (people, processes and systems, culture) to successfully implement? Which individuals would have accountability for which pieces? How will they be measured and rewarded for their progress and effort? How would we rate our readiness for execution?

Red _____ Yellow _____ Green _____

What specific action can we take to improve execution? _____

◎ People and Culture

What aspects of our culture will help us implement customized teaching and learning and which aspects will hurt us? What is our attitude toward risk and innovation? What skill gaps must be filled and how will we fill them? Do we have an effective mix of personality types on our team? What level of commitment, resources, and priority do we have from key decision makers and from working teams?

How would we rate our readiness of people and culture?

Red _____ Yellow _____ Green _____

What specific action can we take to improve the readiness of people and culture?

FRAMEWORK FOR CHANGE

by Patricia Peel

○ Connection to *inevitable*

Chuck and Bea challenge the educational community to think about schooling in a radically different way. The authors view customized teaching and learning as inevitable but they also recognize the shift as a significant change from "teaching as usual." They challenge us to move beyond a mere tinkering with the system to accomplishing "meaningful, impactful, transformational educational change." While many educators respond positively to the "what" that Chuck and Bea's propose, it's the "how" that raises questions. Just how do leaders plan, facilitate, and maintain the change process to move beyond "teaching as usual" to customized teaching and learning?

○ Primary Topic

Leadership, Teaching and Learning

○ Primary Audience

This resource is intended for individuals responsible for planning, implementing and sustaining transformational change around customized teaching and learning including superintendents, principals, instructional leaders, and teacher leaders.

○ Purpose

The purpose of this resource is to provide courageous educational leaders with a reflective process featuring levels of nested learning[1] by which to plan, implement and sustain transformational change. When facilitated in a professional learning community (PLC) context, the reflective process produces especially powerful outcomes. One outcome of the reflective process is its positive impact on the PLC. By the very nature of group reflection, the PLC is strengthened because, "It is in reflection that learning takes place."[1] This is particularly true for adult learners. A second outcome is the resulting nested levels framework that has potential to guide deep-rooted change. As a result of the PLC collaboration, the group owns the framework content; therefore, the odds of successful planning, implementation and sustaining the customized teaching and learning vision are dramatically increased.

◎ Rationale

The collaborative group reflection process is well-aligned with current research and best practice promoting PLCs. One of your leadership challenges is to unite staff members around a common customized learning vision so they can ultimately function as an effective implementation team. Keep in mind that many staff will view this shift as second level change, one that dramatically shifts the system in a radically new direction as compared to making first level change or minor tweaks[2]. The move to a dramatically new direction may well cause fear and anxiety. Just as leaders have questions about the "how" of customized teaching and learning, teachers will have many of the same questions, and more. As the leader, you do not have to figure out the answers alone. Instead, facilitate a reflective group process using the nested levels to frame customized teaching and learning on a continuum ranging from mission to classroom environment. The answer to the "how" question will emerge as the PLC engages in the reflective process. The resulting framework becomes a planning and implementation guide. Over time, as the shift to customized teaching and learning is sustained, the framework may be tweaked as data, assessments, and new research indicate.

◎ Process for Use

Framework

Based on their *Adaptive Schools* work, Garmston and Wellman[1] offer us a reflection process that includes multiple levels of nested learning. For our purposes, we will apply the nested levels as a helpful tool to frame the customized learning teacher's role. The table below lists the six levels of nested learning (left column) along with some clarifying questions (middle column) that, when answered, provide a framework for your customized teaching and learning journey. I have provided some customized learning-related examples in the last column as discussion starters.

LEVELS OF NESTED LEARNING	PROCESSING QUESTIONS	CUSTOMIZED LEARNING POSSIBILITIES
Mission	What am I working toward? What are we creating or aiming to achieve?	>Use today's tools to personalize and individualize learning for all students every day
Identity	How do I hope to contribute? What is my role?	>Facilitator of customized learning >Lifelong inquirer and learner
Values/Beliefs	What do I believe about or value in this work?	>Learners learn at different rates and in different styles >Teachers create the conditions for learner success

Capabilities/Strategies/ Mental Maps	<u>How</u> do I or will I accomplish this work? .	>Constructivist theory guides instruction and practice >Relationships are crucial to learning >Students must be met at their readiness level and content must be intentionally provided
Behaviors/Skills	What do I do to advance this work?	>Aligning learning concepts with learner interests >Coaching, mentoring, and providing formative feedback >Organizing and managing group social networking
Environment	What structures and physical surroundings support this work?	>Station areas including designation for individual work; small group; and large group >Computer hardware accessibility and wireless availability >Flexible time structures

Each level (moving from the environment upward to the mission) "is more abstract with each increasing level having a greater degree of importance on the individual or system."[2] That is not to say environment is not important; just the opposite, it is extremely important. But, while it is necessary, if you only attend to the environment (the individual classroom), the necessary paradigm shift from industrial age to the age of empowerment will never take place.

Consider the following statement: Teachers and administrators tend, by general nature, to be action-oriented. Give us a problem, whether it is classroom, school or district-based, and we will solve it. That is what teachers and administrators do all day long, week after week, year after year; and we are darn good at it! Our problem-solving typically takes place in rapid-fire sequence at the environment level. We are so caught up in the day-to-day that we infrequently reflect on our mission, identity, and values or beliefs. Expectedly, some educators bristle at spending time on theory and can become impatient with an extended discussion at that particular nested level. Even so, Garmston and Wellman[1] recommend attention to each level and caution that, without a thorough examination and clarification of each, a PLC will not reach its full potential. Without doing the hard work, hearts and minds will not change. This shift has to take place if we are going to make the break from "teaching as usual." Consider the nested levels framework as a guide for advancing from first level tweaking to significant second level systemic change.

○ Process

Armed with the nested levels framework, you are <u>almost</u> ready to guide your PLC through a process to building understanding about and to plan for the implementation of customized teaching and learning. But first, your PLC needs the opportunity to build background knowledge through an ***inevitable*** book study. Fieldbook resources to support this effort include *A Book Study For Growing a Shared Vision* and the *Book Study Tool*. After completing the book study discussion, your PLC is ready to engage in levels of nested learning reflection process.

- Depending on the size of your overall group, you will need to break into smaller groups to provide for active participation by all members. Clearly articulate, in advance of beginning any small group work, the process by which the small group feedback will be synthesized and shared with the large group. The final nested levels document needs to be the result of a collaborative, reflective, and transparent process.
- If multiple small groups will be engaged in the reflective process, as the overall leader you will need to meet in advance with small group facilitators regarding process and procedures.
- Once the small group input is synthesized, a draft document can be shared with the large group for their review. After the opportunity for input and revision, a final draft can be submitted to the whole group for adoption by consensus.

○ Story

I had the good fortune to collaborate with Dr. Liz Venenga[3], who drew heavily on the Garmston and Wellman work as she planned and implemented an elementary literacy program in a large mid-western district. Her leadership and innovation have served as a model for others and provided me with a firsthand opportunity to observe the levels of nested learning's power as a group reflective process tool, as an individual reflection tool, and as a framework for change.

Following that opportunity, I worked in another mid-western school district where we launched a literacy initiative that began with identified elementary teacher leaders who were given the opportunity to form a content-specific PLC. The nested levels were used to plan and guide the teacher leaders' efforts. Once the literacy leaders were established as a PLC, guided by the nested levels framework, we used the same model to build consensus regarding literacy in the broader K-5 setting relying on a process similar to the one outlined above. The resulting document became the foundation for ensuing literacy efforts across the elementary grades and schools. It is the lens through which literacy curriculum, instruction, and assessment decisions are viewed as well as the framework for charting and sustaining the course of change. The same process was initiated in the elementary math content area.

○ Going Forward

Over time and with repeated use, the levels of nested learning have become a trusted mental model for me. When wrestling with a problem, particularly one that may be systemic, I find myself pondering at which level the breakdown is taking place. For example, an initiative may have a clear mission with teachers understanding their identity and beliefs but lacking the necessary skills required for implementation. In this case, appropriate staff development may resolve the problem. In another scenario, a review of the levels might indicate that the breakdown is at the classroom level because some equipment is needed to accomplish the task. If all the other levels are aligned, providing the equipment will resolve the problem. It may be obvious that the most challenging scenario would reveal a problem at the mission or identity levels. Cases like this call for "going back to the drawing board" and building consensus around higher level issues (mission, identify, values/beliefs) before making any changes in the lower levels (capabilities, behaviors/skills, environment).

As you strategize a move toward customized teaching and learning, consider how the nested levels of learning framework can strengthen your plan. Without accomplishing this important work, which often involves second level change, the rest becomes a Band-Aid that is likely to fall off.

○ References

[1]Garmston, R. & Wellman, B. (2009). *The adaptive school: A sourcebook for developing collaborative groups, 2nd ed.* Norwood, MA: Christopher-Gordon.

[2]Marzano, R. J., McNulty, B. A., & Waters, T. (2005). *School leadership that works: From research to results.* Alexandra, VA: Association for Supervision and Curriculum Development.

[3]Venenga, E. (2008). *Contexts and practices of a South Dakota school district's literacy organizational change: A case study.* Omaha, NE: UMI: Dissertation Publication.

RECRUITING AND HIRING

by Nancy Hall

◎ Connection with *inevitable*

It can be challenging to implement a customized delivery system for learning. It requires empowered teachers who are innovative and unafraid of risks. It relies upon teachers to use educational research, accepted theory, and expert opinion. It requires teachers to be keen observers to identify the successful experiences that enhanced their students' learning. Hopefully, you have a critical mass of teachers like this on your staff already. To fully implement the customized learning vision, you will need more.

◎ Primary Topic

Leadership, Human Resources

◎ Primary Audience

Principals, Superintendents, and Human Resource Directors

Teaching vacancies typically arrive with little notice: A teacher becomes ill and needs a replacement; a resignation arrives in July as a family is transferred; the enrollment surges two weeks before the opening of a school year and the superintendent authorizes a new position. Wanting to fill the vacancy as quickly as possible, administrators launch into action to advertise and begin the search process. Where was that advertisement we used the last time? Can't we just "tweak" it a little and get it out there ASAP?!

◎ Purpose

To support the district's implementation of customized learning, every new hire is a critical opportunity. It is very challenging to change and shape educators' belief systems. It is costly to train teachers in new skills and develop their knowledge as professionals. You need to hire a teacher who is as closely matched to the MCL vision as possible. This field book item is your tool kit to recruit and hire such teachers.

○ Rationale

Implementing a mass customized delivery system for learning requires unique teacher beliefs, knowledge, and skills. Chuck and Bea describe these attributes in Chapter 5 as "the baby." Teachers who demonstrate the beliefs, knowledge and skills that Chuck and Bea describe are able to create the conditions that support intrinsic motivation. This fieldbook resource aligns the unique beliefs, knowledge, and skills listed below to advertising, a teacher application, interview questions, and reference checking.

○ Beliefs

B1 Belief that learners learn at different rates

B2 Belief that teachers are empowered to create the conditions for learner success

○ Knowledge

K1 Knowledge of how to match learning styles to fit individual learners

K2 Knowledge of how learning outcomes can be demonstrated in different ways

K3 Knowledge and skill in teaching the reasoning process

○ Skill

S1 Skill in aligning learning concepts with learner interests

S2 Skill in coaching, mentoring, and providing formative feedback

S3 Skill in designing and evaluating learning experiences in real-life contexts

S4 Skill in relating to learners

S5 Skill in designing and facilitating cooperative learning groups

S6 Skill in the effective use of technology as a teaching tool

○ Process for Use

Most likely your district already has a standardized hiring process for teachers. If that is the case, you can use this resource as a supplement, partial replacement, or as a springboard for a meaningful revision. If your district does not have a standardized hiring process for teachers, the material in this resource can be used to form the basis of development of a hiring system.

○ Marketing and Advertising

An advertisement of the position opening is the first notice that your district and school are unique. The advertisement should include your mission, vision, and core beliefs about learning. A well-developed website can provide continuous marketing that will attract and inspire the kind of talent you need.

⊙ Sample advertisement material

I like the work in CESA1 in Southeastern Wisconsin. Check out their website at www.cesa1.k12.wi.us. They declare on their website that they are "transforming public education" and their mission is "to establish personalized learning as the dominant approach to educating youth." Their vision is clear: "We *must get learning right the first time, every time." Their statement of beliefs is inspiring:*

"We believe that personalizing the educational experience for students holds the greatest leverage to transform the current educational design and build capacity for dramatic improvement in the performance of the educational system.

A personalized learning system provides opportunities to maximize the potential of all students based on their needs, abilities, and preferences. Personalization incorporates, but moves beyond, both individualized learning and differentiated instruction. There are three core components to a personalized learning system: comprehensive, data-rich **learner profiles;** customized **learning paths; and proficiency-based** progress."

Of course your advertising needs to be true to your district mission, vision, and beliefs, but CESA1's work is a model of what the customized learning transformation could look like. It is an example of how being explicit in purpose can be used in the recruitment of talented educators. Your teacher recruitment advertising would weave together your district purpose with sought-after teacher skills and abilities. For example:

_____ School District is seeking teachers to join their staff in implementing a customized delivery system for learning. Successful candidates will demonstrate (list the beliefs, knowledge and skill from above.)

⊙ Application

The application is designed to screen candidates for the most important hiring characteristics. I find it useful to ask candidates for some written performance items. The following performance tasks assess some key areas of knowledge and skill that align with customized learning:

- Write a learner outcome demonstrating integration of a problem-solving skill and a content area. (K3)
- Design a performance-based assessment for a given learner outcome. (K2)
- Describe how various learning styles could be addressed in planning individualized learning experiences for a given learner outcome. (K1)
- Identify technology tools which would support collaborative learning. (S5, S6)

⊙ Interviewing

The interview is your chance to see a candidate in action to get a sense of "fit." It is also your chance to see if they can walk-the-talk. Have you ever interviewed a candidate who is very verbal and can cite all the current research, but falls flat in the classroom because he/she is not able to relate to the students? I always include a classroom teaching demonstration as a part of the interview. Ask the candidate to teach a sample lesson using a real-world context and problem. Watch specifically for skill in using technology, providing formative feedback, and relating to learners.

In the more formal group interview setting, the following questions can be used:

Teacher interview questions aligned with the customized learning vision
- What do you think are the most important teacher characteristics in building a relationship with learners? Describe a specific situation where you demonstrated one of these characteristics with a learner. Give me an example of where you felt a personal weakness may have interfered with your intent to build a relationship with a learner. (S4)
- How do you set up the conditions so that students will be self-motivated? (S2)
- Describe a situation where you aligned learning concepts with learner interests. (S1)
- Tell me about a situation in which you designed and evaluated learning experiences in a real-life context. (S3)
- Describe a situation in which you designed and facilitated cooperative learning groups. (S5)
- How would you go about teaching the reasoning process to students (problem solving, analyzing perspectives, deductive reasoning, etc.)? (K3)
- What kinds of challenges do you face in matching learning styles to fit individual learners? (K1)
- Tell me about a time when you felt frustrated or disappointed in your ability to create the conditions for learner success. (B2)
- How do you keep current in the use of technology as a teaching tool? (S6)
- Describe the most difficult situation you faced in working with learners who learn at different rates. (B1)
- Tell me about a time when you coached or mentored a learner. (S2)
- Based upon what you know about a customized delivery system for learning, what do you feel you have to offer in terms of skills and experiences? (all)

○ Reference checking

I make it a point to call several references and always include at least one supervisory reference.

Reference questions aligned with the MCL vision
- How would you characterize _____'s relationship with learners? (S4)
- How does _____ accommodate for the various learning styles and interests of students? (K1, S1)
- Can you give an example of how _____ uses technology as a teaching tool? (S6)
- To what degree does _____ use cooperative learning groups in the classroom? (S5)

- This position requires designing and evaluating learning experiences in real-life contexts. How would you describe _____'s ability to perform this requirement? (S3)
- Does _____ have a particular strategy or approach for coaching, mentoring, and providing specific feedback to learners? (S2)
- How would you describe _____'s knowledge and skill in teaching the reasoning process such as problem-solving, analyzing perspectives, deductive reasoning, etc? (K3)

○ Story

The truth: I have made hiring mistakes. I have also been saved from making a hiring mistake through a search committee member's astute observations and reflection. For example, a technology savvy librarian found that a candidate had falsified information in his application; a learner conducting a tour of the school with a candidate observed that a candidate really liked her content, but expressed a general disregard for learners; a community member on the search committee made us aware that a candidate demonstrated marginal professional behavior in public settings. These were all candidates who had exceptional references and who had interviewed well in the formal group setting. Viewing a candidate through different lenses and working with a diverse search committee (student, community member, teacher, and support staff) provide valuable information for the school leader to make an informed decision. I highly recommend it.

○ Going Forward

As you make your offer to the applicant best-aligned with the customized learning vision, you have an opportunity to reinforce with that teacher and with your staff why that teacher was selected. You can do this in your letter of offer. You can do this again as the teacher is introduced to the staff, the school board, and the community. You can do this in a newsletter and press release. Take every opportunity to let this teacher and your staff members know how much you value the beliefs, knowledge, and skills which are aligned with the MCL vision.

SUPERVISION FOR ALIGNMENT

by Nancy Hall and Charles Schwahn

○ Connection with *inevitable*

The importance of aligning personnel with the customized learning vision cannot be overstated. It is <u>the</u> critical factor in pursuing the vision. If the leader doesn't get seriously and publicly involved with the vision, don't expect anyone else to take it seriously. Although this is really quite simple to understand, it is difficult to accomplish without an intentional process. This resource will provide the process and the tool to create alignment between the customized learning vision and the energy of its people.

○ Primary Topic

Leadership, Human Resources

○ Primary Audience

The audience for this resource is anyone in the organization who has responsibility for supervision. Supervisors are "linking pins," as they have the potential to link the human resources of the organization together, hopefully working toward a common vision.

○ Purpose/Outcome

The *Supervision for Alignment* resource is designed to prepare supervisors to conduct biannual employee conferences. When focused, these conferences can be used to ensure that everyone in the organization is working toward the realization of the customized learning vision. Alignment of people is about focusing the attitudes, energy, expertise, and efforts of all staff members toward the organization's purpose and vision. The nature of the supervisory process makes this intentional, comprehensive, inclusive, and a sustained effort.

○ Rationale

Schools and school districts are notorious for undertaking extensive planning, placing that plan on a shelf or in a file, continuing to do what they have always done, and then dusting off the plan when required to conduct the next planning cycle. The *Supervision for Alignment* resource was designed to give leaders a practical process and a tool to ensure that the strategic planning which led to a customized learning vision results in the desired organizational change.

When the supervisor is consistently and enthusiastically focused on the customized teaching and learning vision, it signals everyone else that the implementation of the vision is a top priority. That commitment must be shown by all supervisors throughout the entire organization. Each supervisor is a "linking pin" to a part of the organization. When one "linking pin" breaks away, no one who is supervised by that leader is held accountable to the vision.

Once there is positive people alignment, the leader can rely on those people to make good decisions regarding the alignment of policies, practices, strategies, and structures. The supervisory process in this resource accomplishes the following:

- It puts capable people in control of the variables that they perceive to be important to their success with learners.
- It moves customized learning decisions to their point of implementation.
- It engages individuals and teams in "laying out their own work" to accomplish the vision.
- It empowers people to express themselves through their work. Empowered people find their work more meaningful and are more productive than those who are told what to do and how to do it by their supervisor.

○ Process for Use

1. Share the philosophy and principles of the supervisory process in a meeting with everyone including teachers, paraprofessionals, and support staff.
2. Share the dialogue-starting questions found at the end of this resource and review the rationale for the questions with everyone.
3. Ask for suggestions regarding implementation, including when the implementation would begin.
4. Ask everyone to reflect frequently on the dialogue questions during working hours over the next few weeks.
5. Provide training, practice, and support on the dialogue topics in a systemic way that best fits the organizational structure. This might occur during monthly school-wide meetings, in learning communities, in building leadership team meetings, in collaborative work groups, in grade-level meetings, in department meetings or at a district level as a part of an inservice day.
6. Amend district policies, procedures, and negotiated agreements to include Supervision for Alignment conferences between each individual and the supervisor at least twice each year.
7. Record the critical points of the supervisory dialogue and all commitments made.
8. Monitor the process. Let everyone know that it is not "an option" and reward and recognize efforts toward the customized learning vision.

○ Feedback is critical to implementation.

From golfing to leading, we learn and improve when we see and understand the results of our actions and change/improve our behaviors as a result of that feedback. In golf, you learn to keep your head down because you know that when you don't, you tend to top the ball. In leading, you learn to involve people in decisions because you have learned that when you don't, people tend not to follow through with "your good ideas."

As you create open and trusting relationships with others, they may be willing to tell you how you are coming across; what you say and do that has a positive impact and what you say or do that might be hurting your cause. Feedback is about listening, watching, and using that information to improve the process of doing.

Giving feedback requires trust and courage. It is good to remember that feedback can either be positive or negative. And usually, positive feedback, when given for the right reasons and in the right way, will have the most positive impact on the receiver.

○ Story

Educators have a long history of being free agents with "academic freedom." If we are to realize the vision of customized teaching and learning, we must all function as one organizational team. Employees <u>do not</u> have the option as to whether they will implement that organizational focus. If that option exists, you don't have an "organization," a "team," or a "coordinated effort." What you <u>do</u> have is a group of individual teachers unified by a common parking lot!

○ Going Forward

Supervisors need strong interpersonal communication skills to facilitate productive personnel conferences. In going forward, we would recommend training for all supervisors. For example, behavior description, the cornerstone of a good performance conference, is quite easily understood, but very difficult to apply. We all seem to have a tendency to quickly interpret or judge behavior before we describe it. Was it Jack Webb on *Dragnet* who used to say "The facts, ma'am, just the facts?"

An exercise that we use to develop behavior description skills goes like this:

An individual sits on a chair in front of the audience and removes his shoe. The participants are asked to "describe" his behavior. Participants will frequently say things such as "Your foot was hurting" or "You were uncomfortable," both of which are interpretations. These interpretations may be correct, but they are interpretations nonetheless. Or they might say something like "It is impolite to remove your shoe in front of a group," a statement that is a judgment and not a description of behavior. In this exercise, the participants continue working at behavior description and learn how the skill can be applied in the supervision process.

In addition to being able to describe behavior, supervisors need to be able to demonstrate:

- *Paraphrasing/Active Listening*
- *Describing Feelings*
- *Perception Checking*
- *Giving Feedback*
- *Receiving Feedback*

These abilities provide a foundation for conducting the most effective conferences. Look for workshops, seminars, books, and training materials which you can use to continuously develop the communication skills of your supervisors in these areas.

○ References

Most supervision for alignment dialogues will be pleasant and positive. However, there will be times when there is a concern or issue that must be resolved which has the potential to be difficult and painful. These conversations tend to move from supervision to evaluation and have the potential to create defensiveness and win-lose situations. Patterson, Grenny, McMillan, and Switzler have written a book titled ***Crucial Conversations: Tools for Talking when Stakes Are High*** [1] which helps people to understand what is happening in those "difficult conversations" and offers strategies one can use to make those conversations effective.

[1]Patterson, K., Grenny, J., McMillan, R., & Switzler, A. (2002). *Crucial conversations: Tools for talking when stakes are high.* New York, NY: McGraw-Hill.

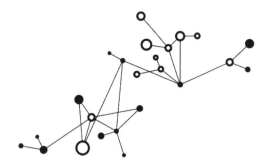

SUPERVISION FOR ALIGNMENT TOOL

The supervisory dialogue starters were inspired by the work of Ed Oakley and Doug Krug in their popular book entitled, **_Enlightened Leadership_**[1]. Research and experience suggest that:

- We get better results when we work through people's strengths and successes rather than their weaknesses and failures.
- Many people are not clear about the core strengths or skills that cause them to be successful.
- There is often transferability of those strengths and skills to other problems and issues.
- Many people/workers/staff members are not very reflective regarding their core strengths and talents, and the reasons for their success. When asked why they were successful, people will often refer to it as "just happening" or attribute it to luck or persistence, without being able to clearly label or explain the reasons for their success.

There are eight dialogue-starting questions below that a supervisor can use in an annual performance conference with employees. The questions have been designed to create alignment between the customized learning vision, the evaluation of personnel, and subsequent goal-setting for the next performance cycle. The supervisor asks the listed question, listens for and reinforces the desired response. If needed, the supervisor can use the prompt to assist the employee in understanding the link between their work and the customized teaching and learning vision. If the employee is new or at a beginning level of understanding customized teaching and learning, the "Teaching Opportunity" section can be used as a starting point.

1. **Alignment**

QUESTION: _"How does your work relate to achieving the customized teaching and learning vision of our organization?"_

DESIRED RESPONSE: Able to align significant aspects of their work.

PROMPT: "Let's look at some of your significant work and compare those activities with our vision."

TEACHING OPPORTUNITY: "Let's take some time to talk about our vision and see how it can be used as a decision screen for you in your work."

2. **Present Successes**

QUESTION: *"Tell me what you are now doing that seems to be working well for you. How does that success relate to our organization's vision of customized teaching and learning?"*

DESIRED RESPONSE: Able to clearly and enthusiastically identify activities that are aligned with the vision.

PROMPT: "How do you relate your successes to our vision?"

TEACHING OPPORTUNITY: "Let's discuss how you might use your successful approaches on goals that are aligned with our vision for customized teaching and learning."

3. **Reasons for Success**

QUESTION: *"Why do you think that those approaches/strategies work so well for you?"*

DESIRED RESPONSE: Any response that indicates reflection on the relationship between practices and results.

PROMPT: "Are you familiar with any research or theory that can explain why your successful approaches work for you?"

TEACHING OPPORTUNITY: "I'm familiar with some research on that topic. Let me discuss it with you and get an article for you to study."

4. **Creating more success**

QUESTION: *"What do you think you could do to apply this successful practice to helping us move forward with customized teaching and learning?"*

DESIRED RESPONSE: Any response that indicates a willingness to explore how successful practices might be transferred.

PROMPT: "Have you thought about the possibility that your successful approach might also ..."

TEACHING OPPORTUNITY: "Your colleague...uses a strategy much like that when he/she...Maybe I can find a time that the three of us can get together to share successful strategies..."

5. Leader/ organizational and support

QUESTION: *"What can I do, or stop doing, that will help you to consistently improve your work?"*

DESIRED RESPONSE: Can identify specific things that you, the leader, can do that will help him/her to create quality products/services.

PROMPT: "What could I, or the organization, do that would make continuous improvement a high priority for you?"

TEACHING OPPORTUNITY: "My role is to support you in the creation of quality products/services. Where could our quality improve, and how could I support you in your efforts?"

6. Trend Tracking

QUESTION: *"Where do you think we are heading as a profession in customizing teaching and learning; what are the future conditions in which we will find ourselves?"*

DESIRED RESPONSE: Can identify a significant paradigm shift or trend that has the potential to alter future conditions.

PROMPT: "What sense do you get about where the world is headed when you read the newspaper, magazines, journals?"

TEACHING OPPORTUNITY: "...is one of my favorite futurists. She seems to have some insights about our profession. Let me share a copy of her latest book with you."

7. Vision

QUESTION: *"What is your vision for customized teaching and learning?"*

DESIRED RESPONSE: Able to articulate a clear, concrete, comprehensive, and exciting vision for his/her unit.

PROMPT: "When you dream about your work unit, what do you see? If everything were perfect, what would it look like?"

TEACHING OPPORTUNITY: "Being a visionary is very important... Being a visionary means...and your vision has the power to...I would like you to read an exciting article..."

8. Vision Alignment

QUESTION: *"Is there anything that this organization is asking you to do that you find contrary to your personal vision?"*

DESIRED RESPONSE: Any response that indicates that he/she has reflected on the alignment of his/her vision and the vision of the organization.

PROMPT: "Have you taken time to identify your personal vision and then compare it to our organization's vision?"

TEACHING OPPORTUNITY: "There are a number of authors who have outlined reflective processes that you might use to clarify your vision...I personally used...and would share..."

[1]Oakley, E., & Krug, D. (1991). *Enlightened leadership.* Denver, CO: Stone Tree Publishing.

REWARDING AND RECOGNIZING BEHAVIORS

by Nancy Hall

○ Connection with *inevitable*

Chapter 10 of *inevitable* develops understanding of how to apply the best leadership thinking toward the Mass Customized Learning (MCL) vision. The chapter describes how a leader works with others to create Purpose, Vision, Ownership, and Capacity. It also describes the importance of *Providing Support for the Change by Rewarding Positive Contributions* (p. 179). An emphasis is placed on rewarding new types of behaviors, such as risk-taking, that reflect today's fast moving, innovative workplace.

○ Primary Topic

Human Resources

○ Primary Audience

A leader's day is full of meetings and urgent activities. When I was a principal it wasn't until those first few minutes before the busy agenda got underway or at the end of the day when I had time to think about the important work of recognizing and rewarding teachers and staff for their valuable contributions. I had maybe ten minutes at a maximum to prepare a note of appreciation, stop by a teacher's room, write a paragraph for a newsletter, or send off an email of thanks. Over the years, I discovered that these minutes were some of the most productive in providing meaningful support for change and motivating individuals toward group goals.

○ Purpose

This field book item can be used by leaders when they observe behaviors of teachers and other staff members that they want to recognize, reward, and encourage as a part of the developing customized learning culture.

○ Rationale

Chuck acknowledges that leaders have routinely rewarded staff behaviors such as hard work, getting things done on time, and having good attitudes. He challenges us to think about providing support for new behaviors that will be critical to implementing customized learning such as risk-taking, challenging the status quo, and committing fully to team efforts.

○ Process for Use

Examples of commendations relating to the behaviors of risk-taking, challenging the status quo, and committing to team efforts have been drafted using themes from *inevitable*. The commendations need to be adapted to fit individuals in your learning community or district for authenticity and sincerity. The more specific your recognition, the greater impact you will have in shaping behavior toward customized learning. An additional section provides leaders with key ideas and concepts to stimulate further thinking when you have just minutes to write.

Commendations can be delivered in a variety of ways. You will likely have your own style and preference. I used them in writing summary statements in annual performance reviews, letters of commendation, "attaboy" and "attagirl" email messages, thank you notes and cards, applications for teacher/employee of the year, retirement celebrations, school/district newsletters, hallway conversations, informal introductions, opening school year/academic term remarks, and board meeting recognitions.

○ Story

A superintendent shared a story with me about the power in valuing and commending employees. He said that he was having a particularly busy and stressful day, but raced out of the office anyway just in time to arrive at a school building where there was a retirement social for a custodian. The superintendent said that the custodian looked up with surprise to see him. The superintendent then took a few minutes to publicly share the value of the custodian's contribution to the school and its learners. The custodian's eyes became moist as he shook the superintendent's hand to thank him for his remarks. A heartfelt commendation is a powerful tool.

○ Going Forward

Through the use of frequent and targeted commendations, the leader has the capacity to create an organizational climate in which faculty and staff also feel comfortable commending each other for risk taking, challenging the status quo, and teamwork. The Parent Teacher Association, the Teacher Association, the School Board, and the Retired Teacher Association are other entities that could be encouraged to provide support for the change to customized learning by rewarding positive contributions.

REWARDING POSITIVE CONTRIBUTIONS EXAMPLES OF COMMENDATIONS AND WORDS FOR SCHOOL LEADERS

○ Risk-Taking and Winning

Definition of risk: Exposure to the chance of injury or loss.

○ Examples of Commendations:

1. I appreciated your flexible thinking! Because of your contribution in the staff meeting today, others were able to begin thinking about changing our school schedule to make it possible to meet the needs of individual learners every hour of every day. Thanks!

2. Thank you! We needed your technology expertise to expand our school's use of technology as both a management tool and as a direct learning alternative for learner outcomes. I appreciate your willingness to take risks to improve student learning.

3. You have demonstrated remarkable skill in guiding our district in identifying life-role based outcomes for our learners. I have the utmost admiration and respect for your work. You are a winner!

Words and related concepts:

Decision-making, Data analysis, Value-added, Outcomes, Explorer, Adventurer, Champion, Victory

○ Risk-Taking, Losing, and Learning

Definitions: Acquiring new or modifying existing <u>knowledge</u>, <u>behaviors</u>, <u>skills</u>, <u>values</u>, or <u>preferences.</u> Extending what has been learned in one context to new contexts.

○ Examples of Commendations:

1. I appreciated your initiative and your adaptability as you presented the concept of a learner's ePortfolio to the school board and led the discussion regarding its capacity to replace traditional letter grades and report cards. While the school board indicated that they are not ready for this transformational change, you left the door open for future discussions. I admired the way you were able to think on your feet!

2. Thank you for being one of the first teachers to experiment with an online learning seminar. Although the feedback from learners and parents was mixed, your pioneer work has provided our school with a quality template from which to continue our course development.

Words and related concepts:
Play, Experiment, Challenge, Unexpected outcomes, Failure to anticipate, Failure to perceive, Hard to control, Hard to predict, Experience common to all, Hindsight, Murphy's Law, Unforeseeable

○ Challenging the Status Quo

Definition of status quo: The existing state or condition.

○ Examples of Commendations:

1. You have a unique way of challenging the thinking of your colleagues while maintaining a professional demeanor and being sensitive to their feelings. I appreciate you and so do our learners! Our learners are empowered and they expect shared control and interaction. Thank you for your advocacy for customized learning.

2. You are extremely tactful when dealing with colleagues who have points of view quite different from your own. You listened and dealt fairly with different factions of our staff while making the case that the information age requires creative and self-directed problem solvers. Great intervention! I appreciate it very much.

Words and concepts:
Changing, Adapting, Diverging, Transforming, Shaping, Variation, Extinction, Learning, Growing, Developing

○ Committing Fully to Team Efforts

Definition of teamwork: Cooperative effort on the part of a group of persons acting together in the interest of a common cause.

○ Examples of Commendations:

1. I appreciate the way you take responsibility as a teacher in relation to the district's strategic plan. Thank you for piloting the learner portfolio and explaining it to parents during conferences. We are all learning from your pioneering efforts and your "can do" spirit!

2. This is big! We needed you and you came through for us in being one of the first to implement the new personal learning plans. I observed how you met with Lori and coached her in the creation of her schedule. You are inspirational!

Words and Concepts:
Common goal, Differentiated responsibilities, Pulling together rather than going in separate directions, Engaging members, Team brain power, Think tank, Solving problems, Rapport, Function as a unit, Productive, Healthy , Responsible, Trust, Helping each other

YOUR WORDS TRIGGER
WHAT YOU THINK

by Charles Schwahn and Bea McGarvey

○ Connection with *inevitable*

The implementation of Mass Customized Learning (MCL) requires systemic change. The sum total of **inevitable** has to do with change. This Fieldbook entry is about initiating change, about an early, low-risk approach to change. The need for transformational change begins with Facing Realities, Chapter 1, heats up in Chapter 6 with a focus on a detailed MCL vision, and culminates with the entire change process spelled out in Total Leaders, Chapter 10.

○ Primary Topic

Leadership

○ Primary Audience

School leaders at all levels are compelled to initiate this fun, yet highly impactful process; but in a short time, all staff members should be meaningfully involved. Success with this initiative will be indicated when learners, parents, board members, and community members are using a new, expansive vocabulary.

○ Purpose

The creation of a new vocabulary can promote openness to new ideas, new thinking, innovation, and out-of-the box (otb) thinking. A common vocabulary significantly increases the options available to individuals, teams, and the organization itself as we/they create a new, learner-focused, Empowerment Age vision for school systems.

○ Rationale

Close your eyes and say the word "classroom" out loud. Eyes still closed, what do you see, what do you "think?" **(DON'T READ AHEAD!)** Now close your eyes again and say the words "learning opportunity" out loud. Eyes still closed, what do you see, what do you "think?" Take your time; what you now see is probably multi-dimensional, almost NO limits. You might see a classroom, but if you are not locked into "educentric" thinking, you may also see a person reading a book at Barnes and Noble, playing an edutainment game on a computer, a youngster watching a skilled adult waiting on a customer at Starbucks, a young girl learning how to hit a fast-pitch softball, a teenager taking apart a Briggs and Stratton motor from a lawnmower . . . should I go on?

"Classroom" and "Learning Opportunity" could actually be thought of as synonyms. After all, isn't the "classroom" a "learning opportunity?" Well, yes it is, but it is only one of many learning opportunities. Simply using the more expansive, open term can get us "otb." And that's a good thing!

Try some other combinations to discover how words can limit or expand your thinking and your options. How about "student" and "learner," how about "schools" and "learning communities." How about you doing one yourself? Let me give you the first word and you create the second, more open and expansive word. Let the first word be "textbook," . . . now give me another word that encompasses "textbook" but opens your thinking and options to include much more than "textbooks." Hint, hint, think Google, think Wikipedia, think Apple Apps, think a discussion with the loan manager at the bank, think . . .

No doubt about it, our vocabulary triggers our thinking. If schools and educators are to change, we can (must?) begin by changing our vocabulary. But the new, more open and expansive vocabulary also has the power to do a couple of other things that promote innovation, change, and continuous improvement. When leaders begin to use an expansive vocabulary, they also signal everyone that the organization needs to become "change-friendly," that the *culture* of the organization is moving from rewarding tradition to rewarding innovation, that if you want to be in the "with it" crowd, you might want to watch what the leader is modeling.

○ Process for Use

How to initiate and sustain this starter step may be so obvious that we need not give you our Step 1, Step 2 advice . . . but just in case, let us make some suggestions. Suggestions, by the way, that we have stolen/ borrowed from Janet and Tom, Superintendent and Assistant Superintendent of the Lindsay School District in California.

1. Put together three or four slides that make the points identified in the "Rationale" above. Be sure that one slide provides a couple of examples of the sets of words.
2. The writing below, by an unknown author, can act as a discussion starter while setting the stage for the power of words:

> "Watch your thoughts; they become words.
> Watch your words; they become actions.
> Watch your actions; they become habits.
> Watch your habits; they become character.
> Watch your character; for it becomes your destiny."

3. Introduce the concept to the leadership team and allow them to experience how the sets of words change how they think. Now if you have some "leaders" who don't get it, well that's another problem.

4. Create the expectation that this initiative (vocabulary change/modification) is a step in helping the organization . . . and its people . . . to become more change-friendly, more open when thinking of what education might become, and more risk-taking and innovative as we work to continuously improve what we do and how we do it.

5. Also create the expectation that leadership team members will go back to their department or their school and introduce the "vocabulary" initiative to all of their reports. This initiative is to impact all members of the staff . . . and eventually the board of education, parents, and the community.

6. Of course, allow for discussion and input. Give everyone a chance to voice their opinion and make suggestions. It is good to frame this "starter step" as a fun activity . . . one that is expected to have an important impact on how the organization thinks . . . but also one that will create more than a few laughs.

Our friends took away from the process:

*   Our vocabulary controls our thinking. If we want to think out-of-the-box, we must change our vocabulary. This IS serious.
*   If it's important, it should be intentional. Leaders must be intentional about making the change from an Industrial Age vocabulary to an Empowerment Age vocabulary.
*   Have fun with it, be serious about it, and be ready to laugh at yourself.

◎ Story

Our Lindsay, California, public school colleagues embraced the customized learning vision a few years ago and used this, "Your Words Trigger What You Think," as one of their Starter Steps. The process immediately let everyone know that change was in the air and everyone (well, almost everyone) had fun with the process. Memos highlighted the new vocabulary with color, staff members throughout the system began using the new vocabulary when they remembered, and corrected those who slipped with "school" rather than "learning communities" and "classrooms" rather than "learning opportunities." District leaders led the charge and ~~schools~~ (excuse me) learning communities quickly followed.

◎ Going Forward

Here are some more ideas that we have seen work well for building momentum around new vocabulary . . .

*   Keep an official . . . and posted . . . list of the "old to new vocabulary word sets" that have, by consensus (or by "dictate" should you be an authoritarian), been approved.
*   A site specific list of "old to new vocabulary word sets" should be posted at each department and each school. The lounge and the leader's office might be appropriate places for the listings of vocabulary changes.

- Have fun with it . . . encourage others to correct you when you use one of the old and outdated words . . . whether when talking to groups or when writing memos.
- Have a weekly contest . . . at the district level or the department and building level for the new word change of the week. Post winners, of course, give prizes . . . how about lunch with the superintendent and head cook in the district kitchen?
- Share the idea and the rationale for the new vocabulary initiative at every opportunity . . . service clubs, board retreats, coffee meetings . . . let everyone know that it is fun, but it is also serious . . . that you indeed want to create a "change-friendly" culture throughout the district and the community. Bottom line: it's all about making changes that will impact learners and learning. MCL is the ideal and an Empowerment Age vocabulary will help us to think in future-focused terms.
- Try to be the first one to be openly challenged about an "old vocabulary slip" when talking to a group . . . open your billfold and present the "whistleblower" with a $1 bill . . . or a $5 should you feel flush.

LEARNER MOTIVATION: DO WE REALLY GET IT?

by Bea McGarvey

Connection to *inevitable*

The reason Chuck and I wrote the book is to promote a vision for education that is intrinsically motivating to learners. The research on motivation and engagement are at the core of MCL. We *know* what creates intrinsic motivation: learners engaged at their learning level, immersed in content of interest to them, gaining knowledge and skills via their natural learning style. Yet we still cling to outdated, ineffective practices (e.g. rewards and punishments) in the name of motivation. How do we get the research on motivation into the hearts and minds of educators? How do we shift their mindset about what motivates learners?

Primary Topic

Teaching and Learning

Primary Audience

This resource provides essential information and a fundamental perspective about learning that should be a starting point for ALL education stakeholders invested in MCL.

Purpose

The purposes of this resource are: 1) To increase among educators the understanding of the research on motivation and engagement, 2) To develop a common language regarding motivation and engagement, and 3) To create a continuous improvement culture among learning facilitators and learners.

Rationale

MCL rests on the assumption that we all believe that students *can* learn, *like to* learn, and *want to* learn. I have come to understand that we do not all share that belief. Many educators have a flawed, out-dated understanding of motivation. Perhaps not their fault—as the Industrial Age, assembly-line structure of schools has been built on "control theory" as the basis for motivation. That is, too many believe students inherently do not like to learn, thus "motivation" is about manipulating them to do what we want them to do. Rewards and punishments are the motivators with the goal being control and compliance.

Ironically, learners come to us *loving* learning. Spend time with a four-year old! They believe they can do just about anything. Mistakes are not part of their vocabulary. They are divergent, confident thinkers and risk-takers. Their love of learning is exhausting! Then...at age 5...they enter our organization, which by the way is in the *learning* business. Sadly, many leave us 12 years later hating learning. The increasing dropout rate in U.S. schools is evidence.

I am hearing Dr. Phil's refrain, "How's that working for you?"

Traditional educators view school policies and procedures as the primary path to learner compliance and control. Furthermore, they consider compliance and control as evidence of "motivated" learners. I question whether that thinking ever made sense. For sure, it no longer makes sense. The research abounds with proof that engagement and motivation come—not from manipulation—but from supporting a learner in reaching a goal using autonomy, mastery, and purpose.[1]

○ Process for Use

The following activities and materials have helped me to help educators change their understanding of engagement and motivation and thus create a culture of continuous improvement and risk-taking...the mindset to move from the assembly-line structure of schools to customized learning for all. The first activity is more introspective for educators while the second is focused on building a shared understanding about the research addressing motivation. Both offer an option for ramping in to the important topic of learner motivation. Together, the activities build a foundation which is essential to pursuing the MCL vision successfully.

○ Activity # 1 Brainstorming: Self-Reflection

Activity Outcome: *Educators gain a more valid perspective about individual motivation—as it relates to themselves and to learners in classrooms.*

Often I do this activity at the beginning of a learning segment with educators on motivation.

Step 1: Individually, reflect on the following question....thinking about yourself.....not about learners or school, but about YOU.

What are the conditions that need to exist for YOU to be highly motivated?

Not just to get the lawn mowed....but to be *in the zone* of motivation....you forget the time....or worse....you skip a meal because you are so engaged in what you are doing.

Step 2: In small groups gathered around tables, share your list. As your tablemates are sharing, note when they share a condition that you agree with—add it to your list. And, note those that would not make your list.

As the small groups wrap up, I reinforce the common theme of "what motivates one person does not necessarily motivate another."

Step 3: Then via large group sharing, I facilitate a discussion emphasizing connections to the research.

I ask them to note the "deal breaker" conditions—those that must exist or you will "check out." I share my "deal breaker" conditions and point out that our checking out looks very different from a 16-year-old checking out.

The following is an actual list from a group of educators. This is fairly representative of what I've seen.

The task needs to be meaningful to me
Passion for it....emotional connection to it
Clearly defined....expectations
Yet...wiggle room for me to be creative
Feel like it will make a difference to.....
Challenging.....but (see below)
Need to feel I can do it
Rested....etc.
Atta' girl....recognized..... "rewarded"
Feel success along the way
Have the resources....
Help/support along the way
People: like/respect them; same spark
People: sometimes NOT!

I summarize the list with the following general words:
1. Support—Resources
2. Interest—Connection
3. Value—Purpose—Worthwhile
4. Clear Expectations
5. Competence—Confidence
6. Incremental Successes

      7. Recognition

      8. Challenging

      9. Choice—Wiggle Room—Creative Component

Step 4: In your table groups, write the opposite of these 9 generalizations. Then, respond to the following:

Which list—the 9 or the opposite 9—describes what schools are like for kids?

◎ Activity # 2: The Research on Motivation

Activity Outcome: *Educators build their awareness and gain insights about motivation from the research and writings of leaders in the field.*

The following are the three resources I use to teach staffs the research on motivation and to develop a common language. They all are saying the same thing—just using different words. I will provide a few key points for each recognizing that facilitators/leaders will provide a number of ways staff members can learn and apply the key points.

- Edward Deci: Professor at the University of Rochester and co-author with Richard Flaste of ***Why We Do What We Do: Understanding Self-Motivation***
- Daniel Pink: Author of provocative, best-selling books including ***Drive: The Surprising Truth About What Motivates Us***
- Carol Dweck: Professor at Stanford University and author of ***Mindset: The New Psychology of Success***

Edward Deci[2]: Points to Know/Understand/Remember and Discuss

- The wrong question to ask is: How do I motivate my own children, my students, my staff?
- The underlying assumption for this question is I am trying to manipulate—not motivate—people to do what I want them to do. (Control Theory)
- The correct question is: How do I set up the conditions so my own children, my students, my staff will be self-motivated? The underlying assumption is I am trying to motivate or support them in reaching a goal. (Autonomous Support Theory)
- Deci reminds us that schools have been designed using Control Theory as a way to manipulate students to "learn" using rewards and punishments. Notice the assumption here is that they hate to learn. When we use Control Theory, we get one of two responses: defiance or compliance. He cautions us about compliance. We are seduced by it, but it is the tip of the iceberg. Both defiance and compliance breed "alienation" which undermines the larger goal we have: for people to love learning and continue to learn.
- When we say we have students who are not motivated, we are implying that the locus of control of student motivation lies within the student and has nothing to do with us. However, Autonomous

Support Theory contends that we are in control of the conditions that engender self-motivation. Remember Activity # 1?

Daniel Pink[1]: Points to Know/Understand/Remember and Discuss
- Pink's "surprising truth about what motivates us" includes:
    1. I need to see the *purpose* of what I am asked to do.
    2. I need to develop and see that I am developing *mastery*.
    3. I need some *autonomy* in controlling some of what I am doing.

- Two great resources—in addition to the book—are:
    Daniel Pink's TED talk. The link is:
    http://www.ted.com/talks/dan_pink_on_motivation.html.
    RSA Animate's youtube animation of Daniel Pink's TED talk. The link is:
    http://www.youtube.com/watch?v=u6XAPnuFjJc

Carol Dweck [3]: Points to Know/Understand/Remember and Discuss
- I require everyone to read Carol Dweck's book, *Mindset*. It has been pivotal in grounding the shift to customizing learning in the research on motivation. It provides a common language. It has become the metaphor for the work. One only need to ask: Is what we are doing reinforcing a *fixed mindset* about learning (bad) or a *growth mindset* about learning (good)? It quickly brings us back to the vision of MCL.
- As a summary, *fixed mindset* leads to a desire to look smart, so the learner tends to:
    o Avoid challenges
    o Give up easily
    o See effort as fruitless or as a sign one is "not smart"
    o Ignore and resist useful feedback, and
    o Feel threatened by the success of others.
        As a result, they may plateau early and achieve less than they could.

- As a summary, *growth mindset* leads to learning, so the learner tends to:
    o Embrace challenges
    o Persist in the face of setbacks
    o See effort as the path to mastery
    o Learn from criticism/feedback, and
    o Find lessons and inspiration in the success of others.
        As a result, they reach ever-higher levels of achievement.

⊙ Story

This is a story illustrating the power that a *mindset—fixed or growth*—can play in a school change process. The names have been changed for obvious reasons.

I was working with Madison Elementary School which had been deemed as in serious trouble—tagged with the nomenclature of the state for a very bad school. Thus, the entire staff was "fired" and only a percentage could be rehired. Caroline, the principal, was new just that year—and so remained. In the spring, the newly configured staff met for the first time preparing for their reopening in the fall. I began my work with them at that time.

During this spring session, we worked on understanding Learning Goals and Grouping and Regrouping Learners (across ages) around specific learning goals for a short period of time—a baby step toward MCL. The session concluded with verbal agreements to begin the work of leveraging the expertise of staff and focusing the instruction. The state was giving them a very short window to turn the school around.

I returned in the fall. We revisited learning goals. The staff had jumped in with confidence and enthusiasm to focus on the learning goals within assignments. And so...."How are you doing with Grouping and Re-grouping?" Immediately their eyes avoided mine. "Well," they said, "We haven't done so yet....We aren't sure how it will look.....how to do it."

Discussions and "yeah-buts" continued until I had an insight: My gosh! You all have a *fixed mindset* about yourselves! You do not dare to try something until every "t" is crossed and every "i" is dotted. You are terrified of failing....of not being perfect. You are paralyzed - not daring to jump in. I continued: "I know Caroline....and I know your Assistant Superintendent. Neither of them has a *fixed mindset* about all of you. You are the ones paralyzing yourselves."

It was a turning point. We often returned to the characteristics of learners—big or small—who have a *fixed mindset* or *growth mindset* about themselves as learners. *Fixed mindset* teachers—when faced with any new initiative:

- Avoid challenges
- Give up easily
- Get mad at any feedback that does not say they are perfect, and
- Feel threatened by the success of others—vilifies them or pressures them.

Growth mindset teachers—on the other hand:

- Embrace challenges
- Persist in the face of setbacks
- See effort as the path to mastery

- Learn from and embrace criticism/feedback, and
- Find lessons and inspiration in the success of others.

Fast forward 18 months, Madison Elementary School achieved improvement status. When polled, the staff indicated that two things were responsible for the gains they were getting: 1) Focusing on learning goals, and 2) Creating a culture of the *growth mindset.*

And so....Carol Dweck's book is required reading with any staff with which I work. I wonder if she notices periodic spikes in book sales!

○ Going Forward

Let me say this again.....with each session that I lead, I am amazed and saddened by the number of educators who operate from incorrect assumptions about learners and motivation. These assumptions prevent us from believing in the power of mass customized learning. You see, many STILL think it won't work because students are inherently lazy and will choose the path of least resistance. Ironically, *we* snuff out learners' innate will to learn. We do that with structures, policies, and procedures that give not-so-subtle messages of how they are "not smart."

I am reminded of a message shared by Larry Lezotte of Effective Schools' fame when I heard him present some years ago. Essentially, his point was, "We are doing the best we can with the knowledge we have. We must increase our knowledge." And so....I begin each of my sessions with activities, lessons, and insights about motivation and engagement. Changing their understanding of motivation with these activities is a necessary foundation. The real change in their beliefs comes when they try strategies which support learners in achieving goals and see the overwhelmingly positive response of learners. As a result, a sound understanding of learner motivation is a priority of going forward with the vision of MCL.

○ References

[1]Pink, Daniel H. (2009). *Drive: The surprising truth about what motivates us.* London: Penguin Books Ltd.

[2]Deci, Edward L., & Flaste, Richard (1995). *Why we do what we do: Understanding self-motivation.* London: Penguin Books.

[3]Dweck, Carol (2006). *Mindset: The new psychology of success.* New York: Random House, Inc.

TEACHING DIFFERENTLY: FIRST STEPS

by Sherry Crofut and Patricia Peel

◎ Connection with *inevitable*

Curriculum and instruction are the "meat and potatoes" of teaching. Mass Customized Learning (MCL) proposes that we prepare this standard fare in an innovative way by making maximum use of technology. We still have the curriculum and instruction staples but the resulting dish looks, tastes, and smells entirely new. To continue the metaphor, teachers will need to learn how to cook using new equipment, ingredients and recipes to produce a mouth-watering menu. The question is, are they ready?

◎ Primary Topic

Teaching and Learning, **Technology Resources**

◎ Primary Audience

The primary audience for this resource includes teachers, teacher leaders, principals, instructional leaders, and superintendents.

◎ Purpose

As you reflect on the readiness level of your staff to teach in support of the customized teaching and learning vision, it is likely that individual staff member's skills will range along a continuum. The purpose of this article focuses on preliminary strategies to support the shift from teaching-as-usual to teaching-for-customized learning.

◎ Rationale

According to Chuck and Bea, "It is expected that high school students will learn 50% to 60% of their outcomes with technology, leaving teachers time to teach those most important learning outcomes that require a master teacher working with a group of learners." This statement certainly paints a different picture of the classroom, the teacher's role in it, and the capabilities and skills needed to support learning. Although the statement focuses on the high school level, can you picture a duplicate scenario at the middle level? What about elementary? How ready are K-12 teachers to maximize the use of technology to deliver content effectively while meeting with flexible student groups?

Process for Use

"A journey of 1000 miles begins with a single step."[1] You may be willing to take the journey but are not sure how to take the first step or steps with teachers. Sherry Crofut, Educational Specialist for Technology and Innovation in Education (TIE), can help with that. She works with districts and individual schools supporting their efforts to increase the use of technology as a tool to accelerate learning. I interviewed Sherry, asking about her experiences that might shape our thinking about school done differently. Specifically, she reflected on her collaboration with a Mountain West district.

Sherry identified three preliminary strategies effective in moving teachers along a continuum from very traditional teaching toward teaching for customized learning. Her recommendations include the following: participating in a book study featuring *inevitable: Mass Customized Learning*, letting go of the notion that the teacher is the sole source of knowledge, and moving toward an electronic format for instruction and content. In addition, she advocates coaching as a powerful change-supporting model.

Book Study

As a process, a book study engages stakeholders in a dialogue that builds awareness and understanding about a particular topic. Based on her collaboration, Sherry has had the opportunity to observe teachers facilitating an *inevitable: Mass Customized Learning* book study. As a result, she reports high levels of teacher buy-in. While not responsible for the facilitation, the superintendent has been key in creating conditions for a culture and a professional learning community supportive of customized learning. With his behind-the-scenes support and in context of a 1:1 initiative (each student in grades 7-12 has a laptop), the book study is providing the opportunity to clarify the vision and mission of a forward-looking district. In any district or school, a book study will help determine "the big <u>goal</u> of our work."

Teacher Role

According to Sherry, the next big step in the journey is to support teachers with letting go of the notion that they are the sole source of knowledge for learners. In the world of customized learning, the traditional fount-of-knowledge teacher role is traded for a new role as facilitator. Based on her experience, Sherry identifies three key skills that facilitators need to cultivate in learners: first, the ability to locate quality information; second, the ability to verify the reliability of the information; and third, the ability to understand the relationship between learning and applying that learning. "I feel the third step is huge in making sure teachers understand the shift. It makes a big difference in how we teach."

Based on her collaboration, Sherry notes that the shift described above requires significant, sustained effort to accomplish. It gets at the very identity of teachers or "the <u>who</u> of our work." In this case, the teacher identity is aligning with the district vision and mission; each in support of customized teaching and learning.

⊙ Electronic Format

Sherry considers working toward an electronic format as the tool to deliver instruction and content the next major step in the customized teaching journey. This is the "meat and potatoes" discussed at the beginning of this resource. It is at the very heart of "the <u>doing</u> of our work." Sherry recognizes that tinkering at this level can raise the blood pressure of even the most seasoned veteran! She recommends a sampling of technology tools that can support teachers making the shift from traditional teaching to facilitating. As teachers become more proficient with their technology skills, blood pressure should return to healthy levels:

- Wikis and Edmodo: Wikis and Edmodo are both examples of curriculum content delivery tools. Sherry sums up wikis as "websites that are quick and easy for you to produce." Some teachers—Sherry included—use wikis to deliver content for daily lessons. Wiki-delivered content can be electronically linked to district, state, or common core standards. This feature allows students access to standards embedded in the content. While the same thing can be accomplished on a website, a wiki is easier than a website to change on the fly. Edmodo, a second content delivery tool, is one of many available for teacher consideration. Sherry recommends Edmodo, in particular, because along with content delivery, it has a Facebook-like feature. It also offers flexibility for teacher grading and reporting.

- Social networking: In the Facebook world of today's learners, Edmodo provides a primary collaboration tool featuring a closed social community. Students have a Facebook-like experience in a safe environment where access is pre-determined by the facilitator. Facilitators, learners and parents/guardians, all of whom have protected access, can interact in this secure on-line world.

- ePortfolios: Sherry, a self-professed "binder lady", enthusiastically promotes using an ePortfolio tool such as LiveBinders, because of its wide range of application. "Think about all the teacher binders you use to keep yourself organized. Imagine that you have them on hand, only in an electronic version. You can still have separate binders for different subjects and tabs for sub-headings. Now picture a student organizing their school world on an online site, in their very own electronic binder." This is the case in the collaboration district where high school students' electronic binders might include tabs for: About Me, Portfolio (sub-categorized by school year), Resume, Social Networking (blogs, Twitter, Facebook, etc. accounts), and Senior Project. Given the school board requirement that each senior must make a pre-graduation presentation to the board, LiveBinders provides a platform from which the learner can demonstrate their competence.

- Google Docs and Google Apps – Google Docs and Google Apps are both online collaboration and sharing tools featuring: word documents, spreadsheets, presentations, drawing, and forms, including electronic surveys and quizzes. These tools are easy to use and allow multiple users at one time. While each offers social networking, they differ in scope. Google Docs allows worldwide access while Google Apps is specifically designed to "umbrella a school or district. This gives the rights to lock it down so that students can either interact with just each other, parts of the outside world, or the entire world." According to Sherry, "This safety feature is nice for providing a secure environment for our younger students while gradually opening up for older students to interact outside their school." In addition, for schools or districts going green, these tools can support a paperless environment.

○ Coaching Model

At this point in our journey of 1000 miles, we have discussed changes at the mission, teacher identity and teacher skill levels. Are you thinking, "It all sounds great but how do we get it done?" Are you feeling like you need a moment to check your blood pressure? Take a deep breath and relax! Our colleague, Sherry, has an answer to the dilemma. Based on her study and experience, she offers the coaching model to support teachers who are on the road to becoming facilitators of customized learning. To accomplish deep-rooted change, the coaching support must be 1) sustained over time and 2) nurtured in the context of a professional learning community.

Features of the coaching model that have proven effective typically include the following components: collaborative planning with the coach and facilitator, modeling by the coach, co-teaching with both coach and facilitator, independent teaching by the facilitator with the coach observing, and reflecting at each step of the process. Sherry observes that the coaching model creates the conditions for teacher success through the "gradual release of control." As a coach, she first determines a teacher's skill level and then partners at the level of demonstrated need. Her task is to scaffold learning, gradually releasing control until the teacher is functioning at the independent skill level.

Sherry's first year as a consultant in this district featured once-a-quarter in-services. The superintendent recognized the need for sustained support and a professional learning community focus. As a result, year two finds Sherry coaching one week a month. She reports progress made "getting teachers comfortable with technology", based on anecdotal data and observation, as follows: "Picture an 80%-20% split. Before, non-users made up the 80%. Now (she states with an ear-to-ear grin) it's still 80%-20% but the technology users are on the high side. It's flip-flopped."

This resource features just one example of a district that has taken the first steps on its journey toward realizing its vision. Along the way, with help from a master chef, teachers have rolled up their sleeves and are experimenting with fresh ingredients and new curriculum and instruction recipes. The results are tantalizing.

○ Story

An elementary grade teacher, who was open to taking technology risks voiced reservations during a coaching session. Her main worry was the notion of finding herself in the middle of a lesson using technology and "getting stuck not knowing what to do next." What teacher wants to be in that spot? Sherry had an elegantly simple and obvious solution, "Ask the kids!" She added, "They already know the answer, so let them help." The courageous teacher (well on her way to becoming a facilitator) presented a lesson using iMovie and the dreaded moment came. She faced her learners and announced, "I'm stuck and I'm not sure what to do next." A student said, "Let's figure it out." And they did! Since that fateful lesson, classroom collaborations have included: presenting at a school assembly using technology, producing iMovies on their iPads, and Skyping with an El Paso school. Sherry believes that the learning has been "amazing using the coaching model and helping teachers let go of fear."

Going Forward

You might consider two other fieldbook resources if a book study is of interest:

- *A Book Study For Growing a Shared Vision* (resource detailing book study process)
- *Book Study Tool* (resource including book study questions)

References

[1]Confucius (quote)

DIGITAL CONTENT FOR CLASSROOMS: BUILDING A FOUNDATION

By James D. Parry

○ Connection with *inevitable*

Once learner outcomes are identified, *inevitable* authors Chuck and Bea pose a critical question for educators. That is, "How is each learner outcome best learned?" To answer that question, they propose identifying options that teachers will have at the ready for their learners. Consistent with the vision of customized teaching and learning, the options may include seminars, lab work, projects, mentoring, informal learning groups, and online learning. Of these, online learning is evolving rapidly and is grabbing the spotlight. As a result, educators are challenged to maintain a sound and current awareness of digital curriculum and content in order to facilitate this powerful learning option.

○ Primary Topic

Teaching and Learning, **Technology Resources**

○ Primary Audience

This is a resource for school leaders and teachers with a priority to build their understanding of digital curriculum and content.

○ Purpose

The core of customized teaching and learning is engaging learners meaningfully for achieving learner outcomes. A range of learning options addressing the diversity of learners is the essence of customization. The purpose of this fieldbook resource is to build a foundational understanding of rapidly-evolving digital curriculum and content as the basis for one of the learning options touted in *inevitable*; that is, online learning. In particular, this resource establishes some common ground for a shared understanding about online tools and products focused on curriculum and content. Clear definitions are still evolving in the education community, but this resource is meant to address a range of language including digital curriculum and content, digital learning, online resources, and technology-based tools and products.

It's Inevitable: Customized Teaching and Learning

○ Rationale

Digital curriculum and content is the elephant in the room when it comes to talking about a range of learning options fitting for customized teaching and learning. Educators know and relate to options such as seminars and lab work. At the same time, educator perceptions and experiences with online tools and products for curriculum and content are growing rapidly but vary greatly.

Virtually all educators recognize the imperative reality that schools are on a path for engaging learners with more online products. And, most educators are supportive of this venture. However, even many supportive educators possess limited understanding and experience with the plethora of tools and products. In part, that is because tools and products change so rapidly. Probably a bigger factor is that educators are simply overwhelmed by the ocean of online resources for curriculum and content—given time and energy in their busy lives. One impressive online source for curriculum content touts over 32,000 resources; another one notes 46,000 resources and counting! Even with meaningful organizational structures and powerful search engines, the sources overwhelm many of us.

So why wade into this ocean that feels so overwhelming? The education community needs to acknowledge that "kids are bored." Do not read too much into that statement. It is not the sole responsibility of educators to engage learners. Rather, educators and learners need to be partners in the learning process. Today's learners come to school with a skill set embedded in ever-present technologies. As they step into today's classrooms, they disconnect (metaphorically and literally) from the world as they know it. Yet, there is a massive amount of evolving digital curriculum and content with the potential to reconnect learners via their skill set. As a result, the education community needs to capitalize on the engaging and interactive characteristics of digital resources so we make strides in connecting with contemporary learners in contemporary ways. Clearly, those connections can lead today's students to achieve learner outcomes more reflective of the 21st Century.

○ Process for Use

This resource addresses three major themes: *Where* to ramp in to this subject of digital curriculum and content, *what* to pay attention to, and *how* to ramp in to this topic. The first question, or the *where* question, is about you and your experience with digital curriculum and content. Some educators may be at an "entry" level. That is, they have spent little time gaining awareness about online resources. They recognize the growing prevalence of such tools and products, but reticence and time have precluded much serious attention. Good news. If you are at this stage, this resource suggests some starting points.

Some educators view themselves as invested with digital tools and products, but they recognize the need to deepen and expand their understanding. They explored and even implemented a few digital products but they look for guidance to help them be more thoughtful and deliberate about growing their knowledge. With limited time in their schedules, they could benefit from suggestions about next steps to keep them going and growing.

One more group of educators is worthy of note. This group is the experts as they are immersed in an array of digital tools and products for curriculum. They, too, struggle to find time and to stay current about the latest products. For the most part, they look for someone to point them toward the next generation of tools. They want to stay on the front line so they can make informed decisions about emerging digital tools and products. They are committed to impacting learning and maximizing resources for online learning.

Regardless of *where* you find yourself among the three groups, it is good to level the playing field for all of us with a common set of considerations for viewing online tools and products. That is, *what* should we be watching for as we explore and engage with these current and emerging resources?

A reminder is in order. There exists a credible body of literature about the characteristics of high-quality educational software gleaned from recent decades of reviews and study. From that body of literature, a notable set of characteristics appears consistently and repeatedly. As we explore and consider current digital curriculum and content, these time-tested characteristics should be included as part of our lens. Toward that end, the following list of characteristics should be a part of *what* we include for viewing online tools and products. That is, an online tool or product which attends to these characteristics:
1. Is readily clear and obvious about its purpose.
2. Provides a user-friendly interface leading to effective, efficient interactions and output.
3. Signals quality in terms of the credentials of the developers and base of research which is evidenced in the breadth and depth of the tool or product, as appropriate.
4. Organizes and/or addresses curriculum and content logically and simply so educators as well as other stakeholders can relate readily and meaningfully.
5. Engages users actively and meaningfully so use is a productive and reinforcing experience.
6. Generates and/or values data which encourages informed decision-making, formatively or summatively.
7. Facilitates connections to a larger community of educators for purposes of sharing, contributing, collaborating, or even publishing curriculum or content.
8. Is designed with supports which enhance the use of the tool or product.

Okay. Those eight characteristics were obvious—so obvious it is easy to overlook them as we venture into the new generation of digital tools and products. But with those time-tested characteristics fresh in mind, I believe we are positioned to consider several additional factors which reflect the focus of customized teaching and learning. In particular, educators should expand their lens to consider whether the digital tool or product:
9. Reflects the philosophy of "learner outcomes", that is, addresses teaching and learning from a learner-centered perspective rather than a teacher-centered viewpoint.
10. Supports and facilitates the vision of customized teaching and learning; that is, reflects a systemic change perspective which challenges or replaces weight bearing walls of traditional schools.

11. Accommodates and/or facilitates additions and edits which empower users to customize curriculum and/or content for addressing particular needs, system expectations, or professional preferences at the school or district level. This characteristic affords educators the power to shape the curriculum or content so it reflects customization and engenders a level of ownership.

One more variable warrants our attention as a part of our lens for exploring digital curriculum and content tools and products. Currently, a major contextual factor in the evolution of American schools is the national standards movement. And the buzzword of this era is the Common Core. As a result, educators are encouraged to note whether tools and products reflect the following characteristic:

12. Exhibits credible alignment to State standards and/or the Common Core. While virtually all of the tools and products incorporate this language, it is important to dig deeper to affirm who and how the work of alignment was carried out and documented. In particular, educators need to confirm that the alignment is valid and useful for teachers making informed judgments about the potential of the digital product for impacting student learning productively.

So *what* is important as educators invest in exploring digital curriculum and content? I contend that a lens inclusive of key characteristics can empower educators to make judicious observations about effective and efficient tools and products. And I believe that this analytical approach and perspective is important for educators from the "entry" level to the "expert" level.

Next, let us shift our attention to *how* to ramp in to the topic of digital curriculum and content. In particular, I suggest that educators invest time in exploring current tools and products. As a support for that process, I identify a few tools and products as current examples for educators to consider. These examples are offered as a means of drawing attention to particular features or characteristics and not as recommendations. Virtually every tool or product brings value for a particular purpose. Likewise, no product is a silver bullet addressing every curriculum or content need. Thus, each tool or product needs to be viewed in the context of its purpose and its alignment with specific needs of respective learners, classrooms, schools, or districts.

Also, viewing and considering tools and products is more of an apples-to-oranges process than it is an apples-to-apples process. Some products are narrow, yet powerful in application. Other products are broad and deep in addressing curriculum and content. Some are designed specifically for direct instruction. Others are structured for inquiry-based projects. Some permit a limited amount of customization. Others are extremely flexible and customizable. Some include an informal vetting process. Others are vetted more thoroughly. As a result, one needs to approach exploration with an open mind. I am optimistic that a deliberate exploration of current and emerging digital tools and products will produce encouraging results. At a minimum, I am confident the experience will grow the knowledge of users of all levels—entry, invested, or expert.

For those at an entry level, a good starting point may be the exploration of sites that offer alternatives to traditional curriculum and content materials. Currently, cK-12 Flexbooks (http://www.ck12.org/flexbook/) is a popular website. This no-cost site empowers educators to build their own electronic textbooks by selecting chapters from a library of online materials. The chapters are saved as an electronic textbook file which can be accessed readily by students. The flexbook offers an alternative to students hauling around expensive, heavy textbooks. For a reluctant teacher, this could be a small step toward customized teaching and learning whereby the teacher ventures into an alternative instructional material in a comfortable manner. For a more progressive teacher, the flexbook could be just one component of a mix of online resources for students to access for course content and activities.

Even though an initial exploration may be overwhelming, a guided tour of a source such as Thinkfinity (http://www.thinkfinity.org/) would afford an entry level user to sense the potential of a rich source of digital curriculum and content. Higher level users (invested and expert) could come alongside an entry level user to guide them to a few key Thinkfinity resources which address a designated subject area and grade level. A well-structured, simple tour could build the vision of entry level users for the potential of such tools as a powerful resource for customizing teaching and learning.

The invested users are encouraged to become proficient users of no-cost websites such as Thinkfinity and Curriki (http://www.curriki.org/). In both cases, the sites are rich and deep with online curriculum and content to support teaching and engage learners meaningfully. Their search engines are powerful—effective and efficient. Both resources empower educators to customize in a manner that reflects the vision of *inevitable*. Another resource for invested users may be the no-cost Open Education Resources Commons (OERCommons) at http://www.orecommons.org/. It houses a vast compilation of online tools and products with the twist that users may contribute to the site. Engaging invested users with resources such as those noted offers tremendous fodder for productive exploration.

The expert users should check out tools such as no-cost Live Binders (http://www.livebinders.com/). Live Binders assumes that users possess a collection of digital resources and could benefit from a structure for housing and organizing those resources. Also, experts should explore no-cost Gooru (http://goorulearning.org/). Currently, it is at the front edge of the digital curriculum curve. It is a strong example of a tool that reflects more and more of the characteristics of *what* to look for in tools and products. While the current version offers an impressive range of digital content and instructional support tools, I anticipate subsequent versions will offer a compelling picture of the next generation of digital curriculum tools.

A unique no-cost resource for users of all levels to explore is the Learning Registry (http://www.learningregistry.org/). Developers describe it as a "movement" rather than a website or repository. A joint effort of the U.S. Departments Education and Defense, it encourages the exchange of data about digital content so the knowledge base about such is expanded constructively. The site is one place to stay connected to discussions about digital content, tools, and products.

○ Story

The opportunity to participate in a recent, statewide conference for secondary school principals brought home some reality about customized teaching and learning. The conference was keynoted by *inevitable* co-author Chuck Schwahn. Principals responded enthusiastically to his message challenging the traditional structure of schools. At breakout sessions later in the conference, principals saw firsthand examples of digital curriculum and content resources. They commented about the limitations of several commercial products. They noted the breadth and depth of some massive no-cost resources of digital curriculum and content. They talked about supporting their teachers in developing coursework which incorporated no-cost digital content. It was apparent they were serious when an articulate principal pressed for an answer to his question about how much time it takes for a teacher to do this work. As a principal from a small rural high school, he described his science teacher as ready and eager to pursue digital content for his classes. The principal was supportive, but was hoping for guidance or insight about the pragmatic aspects of course development work so he might empower the science teacher more thoughtfully and deliberately.

I anticipate the scenario shared by this principal and his science teacher is more and more common. He and his secondary principal colleagues reflect a desire and readiness for the vision of customized teaching and learning. His question merits an answer and his colleagues offered ideas for consideration. One suggested a short term contract of a few weeks during the summer when the science teacher could focus on course development. Another proposed a team approach of connecting a technology integration specialist with the science teacher as a strategy for amplifying technology expertise with content expertise for course development during a summer work session. Huddled with colleagues at the close of the session, the principal raising the question discovered others shared his interest in supporting teachers with pursuing and incorporating digital curriculum and content.

○ Going Forward

The interest and emphasis on digital curriculum and content will keep growing. It is inevitable—no pun intended. As the technology keeps evolving and placing more and more powerful handheld tools in the hands of students and teachers, the education community will realize more pressure to address issues about the role of such technologies in the instructional process. For example, apps on smartphones empower today's learners with a world of information and tools at their fingertips. Also, as the evidence of student learning via powerful digital resources grows, the education community will be compelled more than ever to address the changing role of teachers. Clearly, evolving digital curriculum and content present a reality that will impact day-to-day classroom instruction more greatly than any other factor in our changing educational system. As a result, educators are encouraged to model lifelong learning by staying invested in the developments and trends of digital curriculum and content.

DEVELOPING A MATHEMATICS PHILOSOPHY TO GUIDE THE TRANSITION

by Maggie Austin

○ Connection with *inevitable*

Chuck and Bea (in Chapter 3, "But First...Our Purpose") describe a Strategic Design process and offer it as a way to break out of old school paradigms. A first step is for stakeholders to consider this question: "Do schools exist to get students ready for life or to get ready for more school?" Mathematics is a perfect beginning point for this discussion because traditional mathematics instruction has left much of the adult population of this country incapable of using mathematics to solve problems. Their math skills prepared them to do well in school (in the best cases) but often not how to use math in life.

A second strategic design question is: In what arenas do successful adults live their lives and what are the basic spheres of living? As stakeholders discuss the various ways adults need to function, it quickly becomes apparent that math skills are necessary in myriad ways, both personally and professionally. These discussions eventually lead to developing "learner outcomes" for each sphere of living, and each of these learner outcomes is supported by what Chuck and Bea call "enabling outcomes." These enabling outcomes serve as the curriculum in mass customized learning. And, after this, more work comes in the form of deciding how these enabling outcomes are best learned.

Chuck recommends that after stakeholders develop the sphere of living learner outcomes that curriculum and instruction leaders, department chairs, and teachers do the heavy lifting of developing the enabling outcomes and figure out where they mesh with the standards. Usually, Chuck writes, standards and learner outcomes synthesize nicely and smoothly.

Right now we are fortunate because the Common Core standards in mathematics were written to be applicable to real life. *Mathematically proficient students can apply the mathematics they know to solve problems arising in everyday life, society, and the workplace* (from Mathematical Practice Standard 4 explanation – http://www.corestandards.org/the-standards/mathematics/introduction/standards-for-mathematical-practice/).

Let's face it: School leaders have often engaged in visioning processes that have led nowhere! Sometimes what's needed is a more condensed, focused, and subject-specific process to get the ball rolling.

Developing a mathematics philosophy is a way to focus effort and garner support as you transition into MCL.

○ Primary Topic

Teaching and Learning

○ Primary Audience

Developing a mathematics philosophy is an opportunity to bring together school and community leaders, parents, older students, and teachers. Having broad stakeholder input for the school's mathematics philosophy creates energy and commitment for the challenging work that will be required to implement it.

○ Purpose

You have to know where you're headed before you can plan how to get there. So often people think they are in agreement about where they want to go, when in reality, they aren't! Developing a mathematics philosophy gives stakeholders the opportunity to dream and to ensure they agree on the dream. It also gives them the chance to begin to develop a much-needed common vocabulary and to engage in timely stage-setting work around the Common Core Standards.

Some districts have a well-articulated mathematics philosophy or vision that is being implemented K-12 through appropriate instructional materials. Other districts have inquiry materials at one level and more traditional materials at another. Preparing for MCL is the perfect opportunity to either develop or revisit a mathematics philosophy and to be sure that it's still appropriate, current, and congruent K-12.

○ Rationale

"Begin with the end in mind," counsels Stephen Covey[1] in **The Seven Habits of Highly Effective People**. He goes on to write, "This habit is based on imagination—the ability to envision in your mind what you cannot at present see with your eyes. It is based on the principle that all things are created twice. There is a mental (first) creation, and a physical (second) creation. The physical creation follows the mental, just as a building follows a blueprint."

Having a common philosophy or vision smooths the implementation process. And developing that philosophy fosters relationship-building and understanding.

○ Process for Use

The work before the work

As a school leader, you know where your district is in relationship to a sound mathematics philosophy or vision. You know how well parents and teachers are supporting that direction. You know where some gaps are and have some ideas about how to close them. This is an opportunity to inspire a change in direction, if needed. Maybe a change, per se, isn't needed, but an updating is. Meeting with your math team and enlisting their help in planning for this process would be a good idea. Developing a mathematics philosophy is a beginning step in preparing a district to develop learner outcomes, integrate the Common Core Standards, and to determine the best way the outcomes are learned. Make sure your math team understands that this task is one of direction-setting that will drive how your district eventually implements MCL in mathematics.

First, consider who could be an enthusiastic, competent leader who could facilitate this discussion and choose appropriate resources to get the discussion started. It might be you, or it might be someone who is valued for their ability to listen and build consensus. (These do not have to be mutually exclusive!) It might even be a team effort of two people.

○ The work

1. Invite a group of stakeholders to have this discussion in a two-to-three-hour time frame in a comfortable setting with refreshments. It's important to set aside a generous amount of time and not rush the discussions. Begin with introductions and an icebreaker ("What is math?" in one sentence) so that people feel comfortable with each other. Invite people to sit at tables with about four to a table. The discussions will be richer if they are a diverse group. For example, mix up the community leaders with the school people. Prepare a list of norms (agreed-upon standards of behavior) to offer the group about how you will function in this setting. For example,
    a.   Please practice active listening
    b.   Presume positive intent
    c.   Question and disagree respectfully
    d.   Cell phones and computers off
    e.   Limit sidebar conversations

    Invite them to add to the list and then ask for group's commitment to support the norms.

2. Begin with a look into the future. This could be done by watching a video or reading an article. Chuck and Bea's *Future Is Now* (http://masscustomizedlearning.com/docs/papers/FIN2011.pdf) document has some helpful discussion points. For example, the "Transformational Technologies" or "Work" or "Global" listings would be fruitful discussion-starters for mathematics philosophy development work. Another appropriate resource is ***Faster Isn't Smarter: Messages About Math, Teaching, and Learning in the 21ˢᵗ Century*** by Cathy L. Seeley.

3. Have table groups discuss the resource. Depending on what is used, develop some discussion-starter questions like, "What did you notice as you watched (or read) this segment?" These should

be open-ended questions for people to share their initial impressions. After about ten minutes, invite participants to do some quiet, individual reflection. Pass out copies of "A Bright Mathematical Future?" and invite them to fill them out, based on their thinking about one particular child in their community.

4. After some quiet time, and when most have had a chance to fill out their sheets thoughtfully, invite table groups to share with each other what they wrote above the grey line. Focus on the dreaming part, specific to one child. Give them about fifteen minutes for these discussions or less if the discussions seem to be winding down sooner.

5. Give each table a piece of chart paper divided into two columns. Have one column labeled "Mathematical Skills" and the other "Mathematical Dispositions." Invite each table to fill in their chart paper based on their members' thinking. Encourage the group to define these terms broadly.

6. When groups have finished their charts, invite them to post them around the walls for a gallery walk. Invite the large group to break into pairs and get up, take a gallery walk to read each chart, and to note patterns and trends in the posted charts. When the group is seated again, invite participants to ask any questions about what is posted. Then invite them to share with the large group any patterns or trends they notice.

7. Next share copies of the *Common Core Mathematics Practice Standards* (see below for a link) and their accompanying explanations. Give people time to read through them. These are deep and complex, but for now, people are just getting an initial sense of them.

    • Make sense of problems and persevere in solving them.
    • Reason abstractly and quantitatively.
    • Construct viable arguments and critique the reasoning of others.
    • Model with mathematics.
    • Use appropriate tools strategically.
    • Attend to precision.
    • Look for and make use of structure.
    • Look for and express regularity in repeated reasoning.

    (These practice standards and their explanations can be found at: http://www.corestandards.org/the-standards/mathematics/introduction/standards-for-mathematical-practice/)

8. Ask each table group to discuss how these standards contribute to the previously-developed lists.

9. Then invite each group to dream again, this time dreaming about what students would be *doing* in classrooms where these standards, skills, and dispositions were being practiced. Have them describe this dream in as much detail as possible. They can choose the level, whether it's elementary, middle school or high school. These classroom descriptions become the basis for a mathematics philosophy.

10. Ask each group to share their descriptions in a Google Doc so everyone can see each other's work. This is the culminating activity for this session. Thank everyone for their participation and ask each person to "check out" with a one-sentence summary of their learning in this session. Tell them that the next steps will be to invite a subgroup of this one to draft the mathematics philosophy document, based on the data shared in the Google Docs.

◎ Story

I had been working with a group of about 25 principals, math coaches, and district leaders who were focused on improving mathematics instruction in their high-need, American Indian reservation school district. We had met about five times over the course of a school year before I realized that we had never had a discussion about what kind of future they wanted for their students! Yes, I can be painfully slow at times! So, at our second meeting in the second year of this work, I showed a video about how mathematics was being used in a variety of occupations. The people interviewed in the video talked about working in teams to solve problems, about the need for critical thinking and perseverance, and about how much the nature and demands of their work changed every day. This got the room buzzing. I invited them to reflect and then to fill out "A Bright Mathematical Future?" graphic organizer similar to the tool included with this fieldbook resource. This began a fascinating journey into this unique community's values. The energy in the room grew as each table shared their aspirations for their students. This discussion became a turning point in energy and commitment for the rest of the year.

◎ Going Forward

After developing this mathematics philosophy document, the hard work of defining the learner outcomes, synthesizing them with the Common Core Standards, and then determining the best way they are learned begins. As you move toward MCL, your curriculum materials will most likely be a combination of online and off-line resources. Many of these materials will claim to be "research-based" or "standards-based" or something similar. Such verbiage is insufficient proof. This is where your mathematics philsophy work will help! This document describing what students are doing will help you determine if the given materials are a good fit. Another resource you might find helpful is the Math Curriculum Analysis tool. Its purpose is to help educators analyze curricular materials as they implement the math Common Core. It can be found on this website: http://commoncoretools.wordpress.com/ Look in the July Archive, then scroll down, and click on "Curriculum Analysis Tool."

○ Reference

[1]Covey, Stephen R. (2004). *The seven habits of highly effective people: Powerful lessons in personal change*. New York: Free Press.

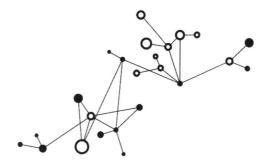

A BRIGHT MATHEMATICAL FUTURE?

by Maggie Austin

Think about a child in our community for whom you have high hopes and expectations. Take a moment to think about their future 10 to 15 years from now. Try to imagine what they'll be like…dream a little, and then write some notes below:

Where and how are they living?	What are they doing professionally?

What are they doing outside of their work time?

How are they solving problems? How are they using mathematics? What tools are they using?

Now come back to our current time and think about these questions:

What mathematical skills will they need?	What mathematical dispositions (attitudes) will they need?

EXPLORING ONLINE MATHEMATICAL POSSIBILITIES: SEQUEL TO A BRIGHT MATHEMATICAL FUTURE

by Maggie Austin

○ Connection with *inevitable*

Chuck and Bea describe an intensive visioning process that defines and describes spheres of living. They describe online preference and browsing history tools like those on Amazon.com, and these help us imagine how online learning might look and feel. Knowing what's possible online is a necessary foundation for writing the curriculum as "enabling outcomes" from the spheres of living outcomes. When planners ask, "How is this outcome best learned?" the authors suggest a menu of choices including: online learning, seminars, lab work, projects, mentoring/shadowing, and informal learning groups. From my experience with schools that are moving towards customized learning, most meet their mathematics learner outcomes in a blended format; that is, they still have stand-alone mathematics courses which incorporate online tools, AND they have cross-curricular projects that incorporate math to give students the opportunity to apply what they are learning in a real-world context.

○ Primary Topic

Teaching and Learning, Technology Resources

○ Primary Audience

A group of stakeholders including administrators and a diverse group of K-12 teachers that includes mathematics teachers and leaders should be the target audience for this resource.

○ Purpose

To broaden a team's scope of what's possible prior to writing enabling outcomes, it would be helpful to examine some tools that are currently available. The process of examining targeted online resources will help answer the following questions:

1. What online resources might help us become more project-based so that students can learn to apply and use their math skills?
2. What online resources might support foundational skills?

3. What online systems are available to help us monitor and report student growth?

4. What online tools might help us with Professional Development?

5. How can we stay current with the fast-changing developments and opportunities in online learning?

○ Rationale

Mathematics instruction has evolved in recent years into an emphasis on students being able to think mathematically and to become problem-solvers. The traditional model of teaching memorized procedures which leads to limited understanding or number sense has little research support. Additionally, this movement away from memorized procedures is being hastened by the *Common Core Standards for Mathematical Practice.* As school communities grapple with some lingering "traditionalists" (including parents and teachers), viewing and discussing inspiring alternatives is helpful. Stakeholders and planners will also need to consider how they will organize their school. Will it still have math classes? Or will all content be integrated? The process of viewing online possibilities described here will help that discussion become more enlightened, energized, and productive.

○ Process for Use

1. Invite a small planning team of math folks together to plan the process of reviewing online math resources and the associated logistics. This team should preview the list of sites noted below and determine whether a math person should partner with another teacher or administrator, for example, in reviewing the sites. Other sites could easily be added, but plan to review the sites in some depth and with a generous amount of time to really uncover and discuss the possibilities. An hour per site is not too much, especially if people take time to try out a variety of the learner activities and explore some of the options for student management.

2. Determine specific outcomes, a timeline for multiple meetings, and who should be invited; keep team size manageable (fewer than 15); prepare copies of the district's mathematics philosophy and *Common Core Standards for Mathematical Practice.*

3. Begin with the question: "To bring our mathematics philosophy to life, what will our instruction look like? What will our learners and teachers be doing?"

   - Brainstorm a list: Perhaps it will include things like the following:
     - Solving problems within the context of a project or real world problem
     - Researching background information for a project or a local community problem
     - Justifying and explaining their thinking
     - Questioning each other's thinking
     - Collaborating online and face to face
     - Sharing results online and face to face

- Building, deepening, and expanding mathematical understanding
- Finding patterns and noticing structure

4. How will technology and online learning help us bring this vision to life? Let's look at some online possibilities and opportunities in the form of tools and/or sites that enable learners to:
   - Invent and innovate
   - Assess their progress
   - Report progress by outcome
   - Build naturally to the next higher cognitive demand level

Key idea: There is not a one-size-fits-all solution. (While some software companies claim there is, it is currently the Holy Grail! What many software companies offer is fairly low-level drill and kill.) There will be different online options to meet different needs and outcomes. Seeing some options will help determine what can be supported online and what needs to happen face-to-face.

○ Evaluating Tools and Sites

Whether the planning team decides to have the committee "divide and conquer" or to view sites and tools as a group, each person needs a review sheet with these features to consider:
- What would this program help us do?
- How would this program limit us?
- Is there some way or some part of this program that could be used?
- What could be adapted, if anything?
- For games…
  - o Does this game foster and develop mathematical understanding, demand strategizing, build foundational skills, or is it fairly mindless drill and kill?
  - o Is there a way for teachers to easily track progress/performance?
  - o Is it more extrinsically or intrinsically motivating?
  - o Do the activities and games seamlessly move the learner along to the next higher challenge level?
- What are the teacher preparation and professional development implications for each of the tools?
- How can we stay informed about the developments in online math teaching and learning? How will we monitor it?

Targeted examples: Knowing your team is critical here. Divide them into pairs, perhaps with a math teacher in each team. Allow generous time. Be sure to try the recommended activities, and also explore other options. This is intensive work and is best managed over multiple meetings. Remember that there are always new sites emerging and existing ones are often changing and sometimes improving! Adapt and update the list below as needed.

A. **Calculation Nation** (http://calculationnation.nctm.org/Games/) (Elementary and Middle School Levels)

- *Times Square* - practice building multiplication products in a problem-solving game set up as an array
- *Dig It* - a slow-moving game that helps build understanding of where fractions would be situated on a number line. Playing with a partner against the computer on these two games could engender strategy discussions.
- *The Factor Game* – use strategy and factor knowledge to beat a human or computer opponent.

B. **Mathalicious** (http://www.Mathalicious.com) (Elementary, Middle, and High School math lessons, with a particularly strong representation at the Middle School level)

These lessons are based on real-world topics that students care about, from sports to technology to health & wellness. This contextual approach helps students make sense of the math, and develop both conceptual understanding and procedural fluency. The company requests $20.00 per month for these lessons (or $150.00 per teacher per year for a district), but has the policy of paying what you can. Free samples give you a good idea of what the lessons are like. The lessons without a lock are open for you to look at, use, and even print the teacher and student guides. For example:

- *Calories In, Calories Out* – 6th grade health and fitness lesson; be sure to watch the video of Ernestine on Slide 7.
- *Big Foot Conspiracy* – 7th grade

C. **Mangahigh** – (http://www.mangahigh.com/en_us/games/flowerpowerlite) (Middle and High School Level) This website has engaging and fast-moving games that help build mathematical fluency in secondary students. Some conceptual understanding is also possible through playing these games, but it doesn't seem to be the focus. Try playing the Flower Power game using the link above. The "lite" version will give you a good idea of the point of the game. To get the full version of these games, teachers need to enter student and school data. This doesn't take long, and it's free. The technical support for this site is fast, efficient, and friendly. It's a British company, so you'll notice some interesting and different terminology.

D. **Khan Academy** – (http://khanacademy.org) (Middle School through Adults) Try watching a math video of a math topic that intrigues you and see if you agree with Sal's explanation of the concept. This site has become extremely popular in the past year and has expanded way beyond math. This site is also the point of some controversy that mirrors the disagreement over the best way to teach and learn mathematics. Your planning team needs to be prepared for this discussion, and an excellent resource to prepare for it is here: http://www.mathalicious.com/2012/02/04/

khan-academy-its-different-this-time/ ; this is a blogpost with fascinating responses that will acquaint the team with the recurring themes of this decades-old discussion. Another helpful addition to the mix would be to analyze whether this kind of lecture-based learning is congruent with the *Common Core Standards for Mathematical Practice.*

E. **ST Math (Spatial Temporal Math)** (http://www.mindresearch.net/cont/programs/demo/tours/SolvingLinearEquations/progTour.php) (Elementary through High School) – Get to know Jiji, the penguin, who has become very popular with schools with large populations of English language learners. Watch this introductory video and then try playing some of the games. There are links to the research being conducted using this program that are reader-friendly.

F. Other sites recommended by the planning team

Step 4 will take multiple meetings to accomplish. The follow-up discussions based on the findings will suggest next steps. Likely next steps include: examining and analyzing the data collected during the evaluation process, determining what other sites need to be evaluated, deciding how the committee will stay updated on online developments, and planning for classroom piloting of the tools and resources explored in this process.

◎ Additional Resources:

- The Noyce Foundation's: *Inside Mathematics* (http://www.insidemathematics.org/index.php); a rich professional development site for teaching and learning mathematics.
- The Buck Institute For Education's site: *Project-Based Learning for the 21st Century* http://www.bie.org/about/what_is_pbl/
- *The Common Core State Standards (CCSS) Mathematics Curriculum Materials Analysis Project*: http://www.mathedleadership.org/ccss/materials.html on the NCSM (National Council of Supervisors of Mathematics website.) This links to an indepth process for analyzing curriculum materials with three tools:
  1. Mathematics Content Alignment
  2. Use of Mathematical Practices
  3. Overarching Issues (Equity, Assessment, and Technology)

◎ Story

I recently visited a school in the "New Technology High" network. I was impressed by the comfortable and modern physical facilities. They were spacious and inviting. Students seemed to be self-directed and engaged when we peered in through the wall-sized classroom windows or chatted with them in the open commons area that felt more like a big Starbuck's. There were two smart boards where students could practice giving their presentations. They had interesting subject combinations like biology combined with P.E. and math combined with physics.

In talking with the math teacher, I felt his enthusiasm and commitment to project-based learning. He shared many examples of how his projects are motivating his teenaged students. In fact, he said, the students hound him with questions about more efficient ways to solve problems mathematically to further their project work. For example, when building trebuchets, they want to know how to improve their target accuracy. When he teaches mini workshops, they hang on every word, because they are about to use the math to solve a problem.

Then he said, "I spend an absolutely stupid amount of time preparing for these projects!" When I asked about what online curricular resources he used, he said he had limited time to hunt down resources because he was too busy keeping up on his own projects. These engaging projects are not being shared beyond his classroom. It showed me that even in this progressive environment, a teacher may be challenged to use the online resources available and that the needs for team planning and professional development never go away.

○ Going Forward

Spending time exploring, reviewing, and discussing these websites should give your team enough experience to be able to move forward with a more informed view about what's possible as they design curriculum, write enabling outcomes, and decide how to organize your school. It's also important to keep your mathematics philosophy in the forefront of the discussion so it can help guide decisions. And, finally, continue to track trends that may give your team ideas worth implementing. The *Getting Smart* website (http://gettingsmart.com/) and blog is a vibrant resource for discovering up-to-the-minute possibilities.

ePORTFOLIOS: PROCESS AND ASSESSMENT

by Patricia Peel

○ Connection to *inevitable*

What is the first notion that comes to mind when you hear the phrase "electronic portfolios?" Hold that thought while we recall the memorable Lori and her 60-day customized learning plan. In Chapter 7, Chuck and Bea identify system structures and practices that make Lori's unique schedule possible. Included in the system structures list are electronic portfolios that "automatically document the learner performances that are required for proof of learner mastery." Said differently, electronic documentation of mastery provides us with an alternative accountability feature. But might there be another purpose for using electronic portfolios? Better yet, what exactly is an electronic portfolio (ePortfolio)?

○ Primary Topic

Teaching and Learning, Technology Resources

○ Primary Audience

This article will be of interest to those wanting to learn more about ePortfolios or who might already be considering a level of planning and/or implementation including superintendents, principals, instructional leaders, and teachers.

○ Purpose

ePortfolios play an important role in successfully implementing a customized learning environment that nurtures self-directed learners. The purpose of this resource is to build your background knowledge about this powerful learning and accountability tool and to introduce possible strategies for K-12 implementation.

○ Rationale

At the very heart of customized learning lies a competency-based system that is fundamentally different from one dependent on the traditional Weight Bearing Walls (WBWs) detailed in Chapter 8. An electronic portfolio is one of the new structural devices that will support the roof as WBWs are dismantled. The Lori's in your classroom, school or district are eager to demonstrate what they know and are able to do. An ePortfolio is a tool for that purpose, one that is immediately available even as you ponder how to tackle the larger-scale WBW construction project.

⊙ Process for Use

What is an ePortfolio?

The use of portfolios in education appears to have started with the development of teaching portfolios at the post-secondary level but there has been rising demand at the K-12 level as interest in alternative assessment grows.[1] Regardless of where a portfolio is used, reaching consensus on exactly what the term "ePortfolio" means is helpful to our discussion. Traditionally, a portfolio is a set of pieces of creative work collected by someone to display their skills. Text narrative may or may not be included. Picture an artist with a large black leather folio nervously preparing to present his or her paintings to a gallery owner or an architect with a file of renderings of his or her futuristic designs for a prospective employer to review. In your mind's eye replace the typical slim, black leather folder, which holds paper products, with a digital container for student work that is capable of strong visual and auditory content including text, videos, images, and sound. The software-supported digital or multimedia container is a powerful learning tool not only for organizing content but also because it is designed to support a variety of pedagogical processes and assessment purposes.[2] In fact, this has been referred to as "balancing the two faces of ePortfolios; one face is Workspace for Learning and Reflection as compared to the other face, Showcase for Accountability."[3]

Implemented correctly, the ePortfolio workspace face focuses on cultivating self-regulating learning, which is foundational in a student-centered, social constructivist classroom. Nurturing self-regulation skills is especially beneficial at a time when many teachers lament challenges with encouraging students to thinking critically and with motivating students to engage in the learning. Process ePortfolios appear to answer the dilemma of student engagement. Students involved in a conversation (process) about their learning and who are explicitly taught metacognitive skills will "think critically and become active, independent and self-regulated learners."[2] While we may be more familiar with the accountability face of ePortfolios, it is in the workspace application that customized teaching and learning thrives.

⊙ Planning and Implementation

Each of you will read this resource from the chair in which you sit. As a superintendent, you are pondering what ePortfolio implementation looks like across a district, in multiple buildings, at all grade levels. You know your district and you know this represents a major change process. If you are a principal, you know that Lori's teacher has a natural affinity for using technology as a tool to support learning and teaching. But, you also know that you have some teachers who are more teacher-centered in their instruction. They may not view this technology as an instructional support. If you are Lori's teacher, you are probably thinking, "Sounds great; just tell me how to do it." Read on; regardless of where you are sitting, this section has something for everyone.

District/School Level:

Helen Barrett, who is a long time ePortfolio researcher, retired professor, and blogger, is currently developing an "Essential Conditions" instrument to help your district or school make implementation decisions. In the meantime, she offers four elements for your consideration when strategizing the change process in preparation to implement ePortfolios[4]:

1. "A Shared Vision for the implementation of electronic portfolios plus Administrator leadership and support." Barrett recommends starting with the vision by asking why you want to do portfolios and for what purpose. She states, "Purpose (and vision) drives the process…and the choice of tools."

2. "Teacher Skills/Attitudes (the hands-on implementers with students)." Barrett anticipates that if no teachers in your district or school are currently implementing paper-based portfolios, a significant "start up cost may be teacher professional development, learning to adapt their teaching to portfolio learning strategies, not just learning the portfolio tools." In other words, if teachers have no experience with paper and pencil portfolios, the learning curve involves both learning the portfolio process as well as learning the technology tool. This may be an example of where consultant support is advantageous.

3. "Technology Infrastructure and technology support." Consider fieldbook resources *Balancing Act: Theroetical and Practical* and *Getting Ready For Rollout: Technology Assumption* for support with this essential condition.

4. "Plans for Student Engagement and Parental Involvement." ePortfolios will be a vehicle for conversations between students, parents, teachers and community. Planning in advance of implementation, including policy considerations, will be essential.

Classroom Level:

Recognizing that ePortfolio implementation is a developmental process, Barrett acknowledges that both teachers and students bring a range of technology competency to the task, as well as varying experience with the portfolio learning and assessment process. Allowing for these differences, she has identified three implementation levels that take into consideration both technology competency as well as grade span[3]. As you read below, picture your learners and consider at what level you might ramp in:

Level 1: Portfolio as Storage/Collection
This is a minimal level of implementation represented by *Collection*.
- Digital Conversion (student work collected in digital format on server)
- Artifacts represent integration of technology in one curriculum area

Level 2: Portfolio as Workspace/Process

This is a secondary level of implementation represented by *Collection + Reflection.*

- Organized chronologically (in a blog/reflective journal)
- Captions focus on individual assignments. (Background information, Response)
- Artifacts represent integration of technology in more than one curriculum area
- Include Reflections on Learning Activities that don't result in an artifact (for example, if a student is involved in a community service project or experience)

Level 3: Portfolio as Showcase/Product

This is the highest level of implementation represented by *Selection/Reflection + Direction + Presentation.*

- Organized thematically (in web pages or wiki)
- Focus on reflection: retrospective questions about the artifacts and learning
- Presentation (annually)

Regardless of where you ramp in, the ultimate target is to actualize the full power of the ePortfolios process. As you define your ePortfolio purpose, you may choose to only use ePortfolios for workspace purposes, you may also choose to use ePortfolios for both workspace (process) and showcase (assessment) purposes. Remember, "purpose (and vision) drive the process."[4]

○ Story

Sherry Crofut, Educational Technology Specialist with Technology and Innovation in Education (TIE), provides staff development support to a mountain west school district. What is the nugget from Sherry's first round of supporting 12th graders with their Senior Projects? "Process, process, process. And did I tell you, PROCESS?" Sherry characterized the evolution from a "checklist" for the senior work products to a "process that is a reflection about their learning." Individual student-learning coach conferences have proven to be powerful forums where students begin to shift their thinking. Many start with the view that their educational experiences occurred in isolation. With Sherry's coaching, their reflection leads to "connecting-the-dots." What initially seem to be random high school experiences begin morphing into related and coherent opportunities that culminate in a product that has learning value. One student put it this way, "I'm looking at the four years differently. It wasn't a waste. I'm proud of what I've done."

○ Going Forward

We began our ePortfolio conversation contemplating a WBW construction project. We have learned that ePortfolio implementation is most powerful in the context of a customized teaching and learning vision, a social constructivist paradigm, and student-centered instruction.

At the systems level: Barrett's recommendations provide food for thought as you ponder next steps. Additionally, consider the fieldbook resource titled *Weight Bearing Walls as Opportunities Rather than Barriers* as a starting point for a systemic approach to the WBW project.

At the classroom level: The accompanying *ePORTFOLIO TOOL* provides fee basis and at no cost technology resources to support your ePortfolio implementation and transition to customized teaching and learning. There are pros and cons to each including cost factors and possible security concerns in a K-12 educational setting. You will need to weigh budget parameters, security considerations, and district policies when selecting online tools. Barrett's **Generic Model to Develop Portfolios with Open Source or Web 2.0 Tools** may be another rich resource for your consideration.

References

[1]Barrett, H. C. (2003). *The research on portfolios in education.* http://electronicportfolios.com/ALI/research.html .

[2]Meyer, E., Abrami, P. C., Wade, C. A., Aslan, O., and Deault, L. (2010). *Improving literacy and metacognition with electronic portfolios: Teaching and learning with ePEARL.*

[3]Barrett, H. C., 2010. *Balancing the two faces of e-Portfolios.* http://electronicportfolios.com/balance/Balancing2.htm.

[4]ePortfolio California Blog entry. http://eportfolioca.org/component/content/article/8-articles/174-google-apps-for-eportfolios-barrett-blog.

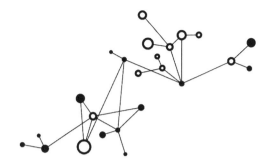

ePORTFOLIO TOOL 1

by Kris Baldwin, Sherry Crofut, and Patricia Peel

Historically, the post-secondary level has taken advantage of free online resources but K-12 application is gaining momentum. The explosion of online resources and the ease with which student documents can be digitized or created digitally can make the decision of where to store the school or district ePortfolios challenging. As with most technology today, the biggest question is typically one of whether to pay for a dedicated hosting system or to take advantage of a no-cost option. Before embarking on the ePortfolio process, consider and discuss the following:

- While very doable, startup technical training for teachers and students is required. No cost options may have a steeper learning curve as compared to fee-based resources.
- If your school or district is utilizing a learning management system (LMS), most have a built-in or integrated portfolio tool available. By comparison, no-cost online tools may be only partially connected to the LMS via a link to the portfolio.
- Students have much more control, ownership, and customization available when selecting their own ePortfolio host or when using no-cost options as compared to most fee-based solutions, whose structure may limit student creativity.
- Consider the availability of and the interest in portability upon graduation or completion of the ePortfolio. Portability varies depending on the host.
- A quality ePortfolio host will allow students to showcase their work to multiple limited audiences and/or also share content publically.
- Digital citizenship becomes a priority. Whatever students post online becomes part of their digital footprint.
- A host that is focused on the creation of ePortfolios increases confidence that the ePortfolio is a safe, protected location that is only accessible via the school's approved user list, although students may also share contents publicly when appropriate.

The following categories provide partial lists of possible resources for implementing an ePortfolio process. These resources, available as of June 1, 2012, range from full LMSs to online website creators.

○ Option A: Fee-based Resources

- ePortfolio (service designed for hosting portfolios) http://www.eportfolio.org
- Microsoft Sharepoint (file sharing resource) http://sharepoint.microsoft.com
- Blackboard (LMS) http://www.blackboard.com/
- Angel (LMS) http://www.angellearning.com/products/lms/tech_systems.html
- Desire2Learn (LMS) http://www.desire2learn.com/

○ Option B: No-cost Online Resources

- LiveBinders (visual social bookmarking) http://www.livebinders.com/
- Google Sites (website creator) http://sites.google.com
- WordPress (blogging resource) http://wordpress.com
- Weebly (website creator) http://www.weebly.com/
- Wikispaces (quick and easy but limited website creator) http://www.wikispaces.com/
- Moodle (LMS) http://moodle.org/

LEARNING AND ASSESSMENT
IN REAL-LIFE CONTEXTS

by Nancy Hall

◎ Connection with *inevitable*

Chuck and Bea describe the community which surrounds the school as a learning laboratory. They envision adults in the community mentoring learners and opening their businesses and facilities for authentic learning opportunities. Regarding assessment, they believe "Students are allowed and encouraged to demonstrate their learning in authentic ways. Written tests are not the dominant manner for assessing student learning" (p. 109). So, to decrease reliance upon written tests, what is a teacher to do? How can assessment take place when the learning laboratory is in a community setting?

◎ Primary Topic

Teaching and Learning

◎ Primary Audience

Teachers like Ms. Lary[1] are the primary audience for this resource. Learn more about Ms. Lary and her assessment dilemma in the vignette below:

> "Students in Ms. Lary's class are producing a video history of their town. Students collect information by interviewing senior citizens, researching at the historical society, and collecting old photos and town records. Through careful analysis and editing, the students create a fifteen-minute film that brings the history of the town to life. This video is presented at the Senior Citizen Center and becomes a much valued resource at the town library.
>
> From this learning experience, Ms. Lary knows the students learned a great deal about history, interviewing, video production, working with others, writing and editing, and, perhaps most importantly, about sharing time with members of an older generation. Unfortunately, Ms. Lary can't see how to assess all this – and she knows that when the state test comes along in the spring, Tim and Sally and Michael won't be able to show what they learned on the statewide assessment. As usual, Tim will be too nervous to concentrate, Sally's reading deficiencies will limit her ability to follow directions and read questions, and Michael just doesn't work well under strict time pressure."

○ Purpose

The vignette above describes a typical challenge that teachers face in assessing learning in authentic community settings. Ms. Lary knows that valuable learning is taking place, but she doesn't know how to capture it. The following resource will guide teachers in developing assessments for customized learning in real-life contexts. A set of assessment tools is attached which can be adopted or adapted for teacher use tomorrow.

○ Rationale

The vision described in *inevitable* is supported by the 21st Century Skills initiative[2]:

P21 encourages the integration of community resources beyond school walls. It emphasized learning environments in relevant, real world 21st Century contexts through project-based or applied work. It is in the community where learners can engage with real world data, tools, and experts they will encounter on the job, and in life.

Teachers may plan to assess learners in real-life contexts to verify the acquisition of 21st Century skills, to meet learners' needs for active engagement, or to support their interest in community problem-solving. Whatever the rationale, thinking through assessment in this new context will make the most of teaching efforts.

○ Process for Use

I am going to suggest four steps to help teachers plan for learning and assessment in a real-life context. These steps are not new; the contribution this resource makes is to help teachers reflect upon how an established practice can be applied in a new way.

1. Specify the performance outcomes in observable terns.

Teachers are already experts in writing performance outcomes in measurable terms and there are many web-based resources to assist teachers with this task. A unique resource that I would recommend to integrate learning and assessing in real-life contexts is the *P21 Common Core Toolkit*[2]. What makes this resource particularly valuable is that it aligns 21st Century Skills with State Common Core Standards and if teachers look carefully, they can find the lesson examples that have already been designed for application in the community. Below is an example from the Toolkit which fits nicely with Ms. Lary's project:

Sample Learner Outcome: Demonstrate ability to work effectively with diverse teams.

Learners collaborate with senior citizens in a digital storytelling workshop. The teams bring to life a story from a senior's history as they collaborate on writing and creating the video. Learners will conduct interviews, perform research using nonfiction texts, write and record the script, and select images and music.

The finished videos are presented in a school film festival. Each team designs criteria for evaluating their video in advance, and evaluates their work accordingly Learners demonstrate the ability to work effectively with diverse teams.

Common Core Standards for 12th Grade English Language Arts

Determine the central ideas or information of a primary or secondary source; provide an accurate summary that makes clear the relationships among the key details and ideas.

Gather relevant information from multiple authoritative print and digital sources, using advanced searches effectively; assess the strengths and limitations of each source in terms of the task, purpose, and audience; integrate information into the text selectively to maintain the flow of ideas, avoiding plagiarism and over-reliance on any one source and following a standard format for citation.

Make strategic use of digital media (e.g., textual, graphical, audio, visual and interactive elements) in presentations to enhance understanding of findings, reasoning, and evidence and to add interest.

21st Century Skills Represented

Collaboration, Critical Thinking, Communication, Media Literacy, Self-Direction, Creativity

2. Select the focus of the assessment (process or product or both)

Teachers will want to use different assessment tools in real-life contexts depending upon whether they are focusing on the learners' use of a process in the community setting or the product which results from the work in the community.

Often *process assessment* is emphasized during the early stages of learning when the correct procedure is critical to the quality of a product at a later stage. Examples of processes you might want to assess in the community are the learners' ability to locate primary source information, conduct interviews, work as a team member, or demonstrate responsible behavior in a field setting. If learners are at various locations within the community it will make direct observation of these performance skills by the teacher difficult. However, teachers can rely upon a well-designed assessment tool for self-analysis by the learner or use a clear and concise rating form completed by a community mentor to monitor and assess learner skills. Several tools have been designed for this purpose and are attached to this resource including a *Group Process Evaluation, Self-Reflection Daily Log, Field Work Rubric,* and the *Personal, Social and Civic Responsibility Rubric.*

A *product assessment* would be appropriate when the product is the primary focus of attention and the procedure the learner uses is of minimal significance. For example, various procedures could lead to equally good products or the procedural steps may have already been mastered and demonstrated in the classroom setting. A *Project-Based Rubric* has been designed for teacher use in the attached resource.

3. Select the performance setting that provides for the best learning opportunity.

There are many opportunities for learning in a community setting. I just looked in my phone book and found several locations which I would consider: Senior centers, the Humane Society, libraries, businesses, recreation centers, civic meetings, visitor centers, chambers of commerce, art centers, fire stations, police department, public works departments, preschools, insurance offices, real estate offices, political offices, funeral homes, armed services offices, the health department, transportation department, human services, and churches. Teachers may have used these settings in the past for field trips. How is a field trip different from a learning laboratory? The following criteria will help teachers consider this question and select the best setting for customized learning:

Criteria to consider in selecting the community learning setting:

Never   Sometimes Routinely **Would this setting allow:**

1 - - - - - - - 2 - - - - - - - 3 - - - - - - - a. learner autonomy and initiative?
1 - - - - - - - 2 - - - - - - - 3 - - - - - - - b. use of primary sources, data, manipulative, or interactive materials?
1 - - - - - - - 2 - - - - - - - 3 - - - - - - - c. learners to do things like, "apply, analyze, predict, create, design?"
1 - - - - - - - 2 - - - - - - - 3 - - - - - - - d. learner interests and choices to drive or alter the focus of learning?
1 - - - - - - - 2 - - - - - - - 3 - - - - - - - e. learners to build on prior knowledge?
1 - - - - - - - 2 - - - - - - - 3 - - - - - - - f. learners to voice their opinions and concerns?
1 - - - - - - - 2 - - - - - - - 3 - - - - - - - g. teachers to participate as a partner in the learning process?
1 - - - - - - - 2 - - - - - - - 3 - - - - - - - h. learners to be curious and ask questions?
(Add up this set of scores) **Quality of community setting score sub-total /24**

4. Select the method of observing, recording, and scoring

Observing learners in a natural setting is one of the most common methods of assessing performance. I like to use a checklist or rating scale to help me be objective, to provide meaningful feedback to the learner, and to have useful information at a later date to look for patterns of growth. A checklist is basically a list of performance tasks with a simple "yes" or "no" judgment. Inform learners in advance of the method and criteria to be used in evaluating their performance. Better yet, involve the learners in designing the scoring form!

Story

Let's get back to Ms. Lary's history project with her students and take a look at how she applies this assessment process to work her students are doing in the community:

"Ms. Lary helps the students clarify from the start the standards they will be working on in this project. For each standard, the class determines what would constitute quality work. As students work on this project, Ms. Lary checks on their progress, records observations on their work in class, leads in-class discussions about successes and challenges, and has students write short responses to detail their contributions to the work and what they see as their strengths and weaknesses. Ms. Lary gives students a test that asks them to give advice to interviewers, to write an essay on the town's history, and to discuss one thing they felt they learned from working with seniors. In addition, she collects and provides feedback not only on the student's final script and video, but also on individual interviews and writing drafts to get a complete picture of how each student has done on this service-learning project.

Most of this, Ms. Lary realizes, is what she always had done, but until now she has not been so conscious about its purpose or how to document it. By clearly identifying the assessment process and including her students in it from the start, Ms. Lary found she not only had a much better handle on what each student had learned, but she found the quality of the student work improved as well."

Going Forward

Teachers may be interested in working together in study groups over the course of one academic year to design and pilot their own assessment tools for learning projects in their community. Because of my background in higher education, I can't help but think of including interns from teacher preparation institutions in this work. Hint: Interns have great technology skills and will be able to share time-saving techniques for managing and storing assessment data!

References

[1]National Service-Learning and Assessment Study Group. (1999). *Service learning and assessment: A field guide for teachers.* Vermont: State of Vermont Department of Education.

[2]Framework for 21st Century Learning. (n.d.) *P21 common core tool kit: A guide to aligning the common core state standards with the framework for 21st century skills.* Retrieved from http://www.p21.org/overview/skills-framework.

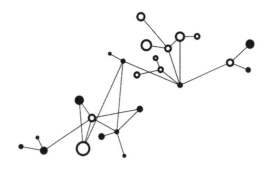

TOOLS FOR ASSESSMENT OF LEARNING IN REAL-LIFE CONTEXTS

by Nancy Hall

◎ **Group Process Evaluation**

My name: _____

Group members' names: _____

1. How effectively did your group work together on this assignment? (circle the appropriate response)

1	2	3	4	5
not at all	poorly	adequately	well	extremely well

2. How many of the group members participated actively most of the time? _____

3. How many of the group members came prepared for the group work most of the time?

    _____

4. Give one example of something you learned from the group that you probably would not have learned on your own.

5. Give one example of something the other group members learned from you that they probably would not have learned without you.

6. What is one specific change the group could make that would help improve everyone's learning?

○ Self Reflection Daily Log

Name _____

Directions: The questions below are meant to help you with your learning. As you respond, be as specific and honest as you can be. After you have completed three self-reflections, talk over your answers with your teacher mentor or your community mentor.

What was the most useful or meaningful thing you learned in your community setting today?

What questions remain in your mind at the end of your experience today?

What was the "muddiest" thing that you observed in the community experience today? (What wasn't clear to you?)

Did you notice anything interesting or surprising?

Given what you learned from your reflection, is there anything you would like to do differently to make your learning experience in the community more productive?

○ Field Work Rubric

Evaluation Elements	4	3	2	I	0
Time on Task	90-100%	80-89%	70-79%	60-69%	<60%
Positive Impact	Makes strong, positive impact.	Makes positive impact.	Makes modest impact.	Has no impact.	Makes negative impact.
Self-discipline	Always demonstrates self-discipline.	Consistently displays self-discipline.	Generally displays self-discipline.	Seldom displays self-discipline.	Does not display self-discipline.
Directions	Always listens to directions.	Consistently listens to directions.	Generally listens to directions.	Seldom listens to and understands directions.	Does not listen to and understand directions.
Language	Always uses appropriate language.	Consistently uses appropriate language.	Occasionally uses appropriate language.	Sometimes uses inappropriate language.	Uses inappropriate language.
Respect for Property	Always takes responsibility for use and care of property.	Consistently takes responsibility for use and care of property.	Generally takes responsibility for use and care of property.	Seldom takes responsibility for use and care of property.	Does not take responsibility for use and care of property.

○ Personal, Social, and Civic Responsibility Rubric

Criteria	2 Proficient Demonstration	I Partial Demonstration	0 No Demonstration
Personal	Able to demonstrate responsible personal behavior, including safe conduct and appropriate etiquette.	Able to explain responsible personal behavior, but demonstrates it inconsistently.	Does not demonstrate responsible personal behavior.
Social	Able to demonstrate the leadership and membership skills necessary to function as a member of a team and to use strategies to prevent or solve conflict.	Able to use membership skills necessary to function as a member of a team.	Does not use skills necessary to function as a member of a team.
Civic	Able to identify and voice an opinion about a public policy issue and to explain the importance of active, informed participation in addressing that issue.	Able to identify a public policy issue.	Unable to identify a public policy issue.

⊙ Project-Based Rubric

Criteria	3 Proficient Demonstration	2 Partial Demonstration	1 Attempted Demonstration	0 No Demonstration
Identification of Problem	Formulates a question with a plan for inquiry that details the skills, knowledge, people, tools, and other resources needed to answer that question.	Formulates a question with a plan for inquiry that identifies the skills, knowledge, people, tools, or other resources associated with the solution.	Poses a question for inquiry.	No question identified.
Variety of Sources	Uses technology to identify and collect qualitative and quantitative information from a variety of primary and secondary sources to address the question.	Uses technology to identify and collect qualitative or quantitative information from primary and secondary sources to address the question.	Collects qualitative or quantitative information from primary or secondary sources to address the question.	No data collected or data collected is not relevant to the question.
Data Collection	Apple standards to properly record, interpret, and reference relevant observations, concepts and details from sources.	Records, interprets, and/or references relevant observations, concepts, and details from sources.	Records and/or references observations, concepts, or details from sources.	No data recorded or data recorded is not relevant to the question.
Validity of Data	Information collected is current and accurate and differentiated by fact, bias, opinion, or generalization.	Information is current and recognized as fact, opinion, or generalization.	Information is recognized as fact or opinion.	Information is not evaluated.
Representing Data	Data are summarized in written and graphic form using technical terms appropriate to the field of study.	Data are represented in written or graphic form using appropriate terms.	Data are represented in a random or unorganized form.	Data are misrepresented.

CASE STUDY: FOR THE FIELD AND FROM THE FIELD

by Patricia Peel

◎ Connection to *Inevitable*

inevitable paints a vision of mass customized learning in the age of empowerment. Chuck and Bea challenge us to <u>dream big</u> for our children. But they don't stop there; they also dare us to <u>act big</u> for our children. At a recent Technology and Innovation in Education (TIE) Conference, a presenter challenged, "Don't think 'old school'; think 'bold school.'" This certainly reflects the thinking and actions of our Case Study superintendent. "I've talked with Mike, our high school principal, about high schools becoming obsolete. Our high school could become obsolete, right here. I'm not going to let that happen to us and I am not going to wait for someone else to figure out the answers for us. We're going to figure it out, right here." While you may agree in theory, you may also be struggling with how to apply customized teaching and learning in "my school with my kids." This resource will support the shift from the theory to action.

◎ Primary Topic

Leadership, Teaching and Learning, Human Resources, Technology Resources

◎ Primary Audience

This resource is for anyone in a leadership position who is interested in one high school's journey toward customized teaching and learning. The superintendent, principal, school board members, teachers, tech coaches, students and parent voices are represented in this resource.

◎ Purpose

Chuck and Bea are the first to admit their dream and call to action are lofty goals but they are equally clear in their passionate belief that we educators can solve the challenges inherent in mass customized teaching and learning. The purpose of this resource is to provide an up-close-and-personal view of a school that appears to demonstrate many of the "ready for rollout" critical elements described in Chapter 9 of *inevitable*. Ten years ago, Watertown School District (WSD), Watertown, SD, envisioned a 21st Century school. Today, its many parallels to the customized teaching and learning vision make it a valuable case study as you think about next steps in "my school with my kids."

○ Rationale

Considering Watertown High School (WHS) as a case study subject all started with a series of "if…..then….." statements.

1) **IF** customized teaching and learning assumes a fully functional technology system, **THEN** a school with a well-implemented 1:1 laptop initiative will have addressed this foundational step in the "ready for rollout" process.

2) **IF** they have longevity with a successful 1:1 implementation, **THEN** we will assume that technologies are readily available, that these technologies are supported and the staff and learners are proficient consumers.

3) **IF** the first two statements are accurate, **THEN,** at a minimum, we anticipate the school will be well-positioned to implement the customized teaching and learning vision or will be at an advanced point in the process.

WHS was selected for the case study based on their nine-year history of 1:1 technology access for students (1 student: 1 laptop). They have addressed the foundational step in the "ready for rollout process." With implementation longevity, technologies are readily available, are well supported, and staff and learners are proficient users. In summary, the first two "If…then…" statements proved true. Keep the third "if….then…" statement in mind as you read the WHS case study. As you reflect, ask yourself if WHS is, in fact, well positioned to begin implementing the customized teaching and learning vision. Or, do you think they have already engaged in the implementation process and may even be at an advanced stage of implementation? Read, reflect, and decide. Their journey may provide valuable insights to inform your own.

○ Site Visit

Logistics

The site visit planning began after an initial contact with Dr. Jutting, Watertown School District Superintendent. With her permission I contacted Dr. Butts, Watertown High School Principal, who worked with me finalizing arrangements for a spring 2012 visit when I spent one and one-half days at the school interviewing stakeholders and visiting classrooms. At my request, Dr. Butts arranged for individual interviews with himself, the superintendent and three teachers (two of whom also serve as Tech Coaches). I also interviewed three separate groups including three parents, three students, and two school board members.

As I met with each group, I set the stage by introducing myself in context of the fieldbook writing project, summarizing the customized teaching and learning vision, and indicating that I had a series of questions to ask about WHS. After a snapshot of the "if...then..." thinking, they understood that my goal was to write about their journey, which has been and continues to be shaped by 1:1 access to a technology tool.

In addition to arranging the interviews, Dr. Butts escorted me to seven different classrooms and welcomed me to observe a portion of a Tech Coach meeting. At the end of my second day, I conferenced with the two administrators, which gave the three of us an opportunity to debrief and for me to ask clarifying questions.

○ Setting

Watertown is a progressive community of approximately 20,500 in northeastern South Dakota. It sits along the I-29 corridor approximately 90 minutes north of Sioux Falls, South Dakota's largest city. The general population is primarily white (94%) with Native Americans representing the next largest group (4%). The median income is $38,902. Agriculture, light industry (manufacturing) and service industry (hospital, hotels, restaurants, convenience stores, etc.) are the top three economic drivers. The community is surrounded by sweeping expanses of prairie and farmland, with long stretches between neighboring towns. WHS, serving approximately 1,100 students, is located across the street from the Lake Area Technical Institute, one of four post-secondary technical institutes in the state. A few blocks away sits the Lake Area Multi-District Building, which houses career and technical programs serving a consortium of regional high schools including WHS.

○ Background

The current superintendent, Dr. Lesli Jutting, was the Assistant Superintendent ten years ago when a year-long visioning and planning process, focused on operationalizing the district vision and mission, took place. Goals were identified in support of a mission "*Enabling all students to meet the challenges of an ever-changing world.*" The 1:1 initiative aligned directly with those goals including 1) all students will graduate and 2) given that learning is advanced with the infusion of technology, we will provide the best technology tools possible for students and staff. These two goals have been the driving forces shaping district and, specifically, high school teaching and learning efforts. It is important to note that while WHS is ramping in to customized teaching and learning by first addressing their areas of highest need (those most in danger of not graduating), they are committed to their goal of expanding customized opportunities for all students.

Since that time, there have been three cycles of laptop leases of three years each. The first two rounds featured Gateway Windows-based tablet computers but MacBook Pros were selected for the most recent lease, which has been extended for a fourth year.

Dr. Jutting became WSD Superintendent five years ago and, at the same time, hired Dr. Mike Butts as WHS Principal, which made him the fifth high school principal in 10 years. Both individuals continued in these roles at the time of the site visit. WHS has an 82 member staff. By the beginning of the 2012-2013 school year, 35 staff members (approximately 43%) will have either started with Dr. Butts or will have been hired by him.

Interviews

Each individual stakeholder or stakeholder group were asked similar questions. The section below provides a perspective from the chairs in which they sit. By virtue of answering the questions, individuals tell their story.

Story

"Enabling all students to succeed in an ever-changing world" is the district mission statement. Please talk about how the 1:1 laptop initiative aligns with your mission.

Regarding the mission and technology alignment, Dr. Jutting responded, "First, we knew that we wanted 21st Century schools. Second, we believed that if we put new tools in front of students that it would be a tipping point; it would force a radical change. We knew that our kids would push us to a different type of learning. Third, we knew it needed to look different, not traditional. We just knew we couldn't just do the same old-same old. But let me be clear, the computer is just a tool. We would not be where we are today without it. It has allowed us to dramatically change opportunities for our students that we could not possibly offer otherwise, but it is just a tool. It is how we use the tool, to provide options for our kids, that's the key. In other words, it's not about the 1:1, it's about the teaching and learning."

Similarly, Dr. Butts observed, "The 1:1 provides a tool for access. It opens doors to do things we could not do otherwise." The site visit provided an opportunity to identify some examples. One teacher shared, "My favorite thing is when kids send me something they've created, not because it's for class but just because they did it. It's exciting when they are creating and designing based on their classroom learning. Then they are off on their own. I wonder if that is happening in other districts?" Another teacher interviewed will be leading an Apple Challenge Based Learning research project next year. I also visited an AP class where the teacher provides students with access to webcasts of particularly challenging content—students may opt to access the webcasts pre- and/or post-classroom presentations. The principal concluded, "It's exciting when we hear from Lake Area Tech that they recognize WHS students because of their skills. As a result, they will ask one our students to mentor a non-WHS student in order to help the other student catch up. This only happens because our kids have the tools and the learning."

Two board members shared their perspectives. School Board President, Susan Jones, has been a Board member for seven years while Tammy Rieber is currently in her first year of service. Ms. Jones identified 21st Century skills as the link between the district vision and 1:1 access. With a rueful smile and shaking her head, she reflected on the nine-year journey. "Two weeks before school started they got the computers. There was enthusiasm and excitement. It was wild! Students immediately rushed to the music and games.

But, we learned from our mistakes and things are handled differently now." She also talked about the controversy that stretched into year two when they were negotiating the second leasing round. Some parents and community members still questioned the value of providing the laptops. But, since that adoption, the 1:1 has become routine and the most recent laptop renewal discussion was seamless (note: The board opted to extend the current contract one year. A new contract will be discussed next year).

Students interviewed highlighted the depth at which they use the technology tool and how integral it is to their learning and study. As a group, the students recognized that laptop access coupled with customized teaching provided them with engaging learning opportunities. One student wondered if WHS students have a richer experience than more traditional high schools because of their depth of technical knowledge. "We just don't learn word processing and basics. We go way beyond that; we're lost when we have to turn our laptops in for routine check-ups." Another related, "I have a friend who goes to school in a very small district. I understand that a smaller district won't have all the classes and opportunities that we have here at Watertown, but my friend said that we are 10 times smarter than her! I wonder if technology has a role?"

Reflecting on Watertown's 1:1 journey, identify two or three " lessons learned" that will position or already have positioned the school to use technology differently, with customized teaching and learning as the focus.

Dr. Jutting offered four leadership lessons: *"First,* don't be afraid, take risks because you can't create a path of comfort because it doesn't exist with technology; *second,* professional development is a part but it is not 'the' answer. This is a journey that was not created before; there is no book written. It's all a path....some run down the path, some drag the computer down the path, and some leave; *third,* look to the team. We're on the path together so I invite the team to the table and we figure it out together; and *fourth,* at the beginning you need to be out in the community promoting the vision. For example, we had lots of stories in the paper originally. You have to tell the story."

Dr. Butts reflected on lessons about students, parents and staff. "For *students,* there is never enough training. Although some of it comes intuitively, I believe they need to advance their skills. And, you need to think about the care and maintenance of the tool; both are critical. For *parents,* support is key because parenting with a school laptop in the house is a whole new world. First thing, we require a parent or guardian to attend a Freshman Orientation before we will issue a laptop to the student. The Orientation is offered over a seven-day span so attendance is not a barrier for families. Based on our nine years of experience, we have tips for them and we have support to offer. For example, some students will isolate themselves, especially when they first get the laptop. We have tips for parents that include restricting laptop use to common areas at home and to consider limiting hours of use. If a problem develops, we will partner with the parent to address the concern. For *staff,* when you are just starting out, get the computers into the hands of staff before school opens. For us, that was two weeks ahead. Also, realize that everyone is at a different skill and interest level, which means that differentiated staff development is beneficial."

The veteran school board member observed that the direction of customized teaching and learning "ties to the mission and the 1:1 levels the playing field for all students." Her key lesson learned is that the change process "moves through stages." "You learn what kids can and can't do to be effective. Also, the staff needs to get on board; we had a major push for a couple of years." Early on, Ms. Jones notes there were some resisters on the staff. "It may have been fear. We spent a lot of money on professional development."

Building on the 1:1 foundation, what are two to three <u>"next steps"</u> to continue moving in the direction of customized teaching and learning?

Before discussing *next steps,* Dr. Jutting and Dr. Butts first painted the picture of their journey, to date. They began with this reminder, "Our goal is for all students to graduate and that we will use the best technology available to support teaching and learning." With a 100% graduation rate driving efforts, both the Central Office and High School Office have targeted providing supports and options for students. This may paint the picture that all efforts are funneled to those in danger of not graduating. On the contrary, I observed the following: while the administration acts on the belief that there is "no floor," they also act as if there is "no ceiling." Over the past five years, in addition to more traditional high school offerings, the range of high school *customization* choices have grown to include the following:

- AP Courses: A selection of Advanced Placement courses is offered on site at WHS.
- "Freshman Failure Not Allowed": WHS educators often talk about gateway courses that, if not passed, appear to derail the path toward graduation. Algebra 1 is the classic example. WHS thinks in terms of the freshman year as the gateway to graduation. As a result, efforts are concentrated to scaffold the success of ninth graders. Interventions are immediate and interventions are customized.
- APEX Courses: Online courses are available for course credit, credit recovery and acceleration (AP courses); content by standard is available for remediation and individualization of instruction.
- Academic Resource Center (ARC): Four content teachers are available throughout the day to assist student, who have failed a class, to recover credit using online resources.
- Transition Room: Two teachers facilitate study skills support for students who are struggling academically. The goal is to intervene with study skills support and work completion assistance before students fail a course.
- Project Hope: Project **H**eightening **O**pportunities and **P**ossibilities in **E**ducation (HOPE) meets the needs of the 12 potential non-graduates. This innovative program, funded in part by Title I funds, is a Project Based Learning (PBL) Petri dish. With assistance from program facilitators and with approval from them and parents, students earn credit by demonstrating mastery of content standards after planning and implementing a cross-curricular project. Over time, the goal is to increase the number of students served to 20.

- Night School: Support is available two nights a week for credit recovery.
- Graduation Coach Program: Two facilitators with social services-related backgrounds provide mentoring support for students who are struggling academically. The goal is to scaffold their success to keep on track to graduation.
- Dual Credit: Students earn high school and college credit at the same time through a wide range of options including Lake Area Technical Institute, which is across the street from the high school. As needed, the Gifted Program teacher is a resource and/or facilitator to arrange and support other post-secondary options.
- Intensive Care Unit (ICU) Philosophy: Any assignment is given for a specific purpose and is important for student learning. As a result, students with missing work need extra attention and intensive care to get the work done. Assigning an F, in essence, ignores the importance of the assignment. Teachers assign an Incomplete and apply the ICU philosophy with the expectation that students will complete missing assignments.
- Learning Targets & Assessment: Local learning targets have been identified and local assessments have been developed. All core classes have pre- and post-tests available online.
- Diagnostics: A diagnostic tool is available for credit recovery purposes.

What you see listed above is not the destination for WHS; it represents a point along the path described by Dr. Jutting. "For us, the next ten years holds the real power of the how technology can support customized teaching and learning. Our *next steps* are in the visioning stages for both Project Based Learning (PBL) and Middle College."

The WHS team appears to be on to something powerful if the student voice is any indication. Some of the most animated students with whom I had the opportunity to visit were those in the Project HOPE classroom. Identified as "most in danger of not graduating," these students are designing interdisciplinary projects that must go through a joint school and home pre-approval process before implementation. The projects are as unique as the students and their circumstances; topics ranged from photography, music genres and history, to weapons and war. Upon successful completion of their learning contract, students earn credit toward graduation based on mastery, not seat time. Clearly, Project HOPE brings PBL to Watertown but both Dr. Jutting and Dr. Butts envision PBL on a much broader scale. Project HOPE is currently program-based for potential non-grads but the vision's *next step* is to take PBL to the mainstream. Project HOPE students are cheerleaders for this team.

According to Dr. Jutting, "Middle College is our second *next step*. It's something we are doing informally, with specific students, but the idea under discussion is to expand the $10 + 2 + 2$ opportunity." The equation includes 10 years, beginning with first grade, to earn high school requirements for graduation + 2 years to earn college credit while still in high school + 2 years to earn and complete a college degree. Another possible equation is $11 + 1 + 3$. Dr. Butts elaborates, "With parental approval we intend to offer the opportunity to a group of freshmen. The cohort will start their high school experience on a pre-set path toward high school and post-secondary graduations." He shared some current examples of individual students who are pilot representatives for the model. Typically, the pilot students are academically gifted. They require an accelerated program to accommodate academic needs while meeting state and district graduation requirements. By comparison, administrators hope to extend the proposed mainstream PBL model to serve 60-75 students.

Ultimately, Dr. Jutting envisions students selecting a two, three or four year path through high school. Along the way, they will have choices including: Project Based Learning, online learning, and traditional high school courses. "The conversation has changed; for us it's K-14. We don't talk to kids about college anymore; the conversation is about post-secondary."

School board members also had great insights into *next steps* to move the customized teaching and learning vision forward. The veteran board member pictures global learning on the horizon. While acknowledging that differing time zones can present challenges, she also sees the power of students connecting as peer tutors. For example, her son is currently enrolled in a German course. In the past, she has offered him assistance with his World Language homework. "But what if he Skyped with a high school student in Germany who is also taking English? I bet he'd rather that exchange than help from Mom." With a smile she states, "My son would like that better!" She also shared that Watertown will be the first town to be Google-mapped and that Lake Area Technical Institute will be the first campus to have internal global mapping. She wonders about the possibilities in context of that cutting edge technology advancement in the WSD neighborhood. The new board member, a former Biology teacher, offered the notion of each student having an individualized learning plan as a means to customize teaching and learning. "We could possibly use the templates already available in SD MyLife (online state-sponsored student portfolio program). It might be an out-there concept, but maybe we could start with math first and see how that goes."

What are the <u>challenges</u> or roadblocks in your path? Specifically, discuss how <u>Weight Bearing Walls</u> <u>(WBW)</u> influence your journey.

It is of interest to note that overall, no one interviewed identified WBWs as complete barriers to their vision of implementing customized teaching and learning. Rather, WBWs were viewed one of two ways, 1) leave the WBW as a supporting structure or 2) identify a WBW work-around.

Board members and administrators unanimously agreed that the ABC grades WBW can or need to remain in place. First, according to a board member, Pass/Fail had been tried previously and was not successful. "It didn't fly in the community. Parents were concerned that kids would not compete if letter grades were not available. We won't do that again." The Office representatives viewed grades as a post-secondary requirement and not a barrier to their customization efforts. Report cards were another WBW that was viewed as a non-issue from their perspective.

Work-arounds were sorted into two categories. Some work-arounds have been successfully implemented and are transparent while other work-arounds are in the research and development (R & D) stage. Those viewed as working transparently include: grade levels, paper and pencil, and, to a degree, courses and curriculum (when viewed as a range of options).

R & D work-arounds include the following: textbooks, students assigned to classrooms, class periods/bell schedules, and courses and curriculum. Both administrators concurred and re-iterated that the items in this category are all in play and under construction in WHS.

Textbooks - For example, textbooks on CD are in use but that is still very traditional content delivery, albeit electronic. The PBL pilot is an example of a dramatic move toward both textbook and course/curriculum customization. Individualization of non-textbook content is also part of the ARC, Transition Room and Night School Program.

Scheduling - Administrators identified the absence of software to support student-initiated and managed-scheduling as a primary barrier. According to Dr. Butts, "When our students can create 'Lori's schedule' on their own, we will be light years ahead."

Courses/Curriculum - Dr. Jutting views the next leap forward happening in tandem with figuring out how to align and then track mastery of standards in context of the PBL model. In the interim, content individualized through credit recovery programs and Academic Resource Center support are examples of customized content and learning.

In addition to the WBWs just discussed, additional areas needing work-arounds were identified:

Policy - Dr. Butts and Dr. Jutting cited state policy limitations. Currently, the state links standards to specific courses/course titles. PBL is not specific course-or title-based. Rather it links standards to mastery. The course/title structure creates a PBL challenge because a project integrates traditionally separate content standard areas. In addition, it integrates content from several different courses and different disciplines overlap. Project HOPE is providing the high school with an R & D field laboratory to explore possibilities.

Budget - Each person referenced budget constraints as a challenge but also refused to view it as a "deal breaker." For example, the Middle College concept under discussion includes post-secondary course costs. Preliminary conversations will need to include innovative funding options.

Language - The superintendent and board members highlighted the need for community-friendly language when communicating with non-educator stakeholders. Each stressed the importance of framing conversations about innovations and bleeding-edge reforms in familiar terms. Failing to do so can create unintended barriers.

From where you sit, what is the greatest challenge for teaching staff making the shift to customized teaching and learning? How can you best support teachers in that journey?

The principal discussed the challenge of promoting a culture where instruction and philosophy are aligned. "I view myself as the key communicator supporting teachers to make the shift, to run with being the facilitator. My role is to help them figure out what they need to keep and what students can do alone. 25% run with it, 50% are transitioning but tend to be traditional, and 25% are only using the tool for attendance. Recognizing teachers are at different points on their journey toward becoming facilitators, he believes sustained professional development (PD) is the answer. Key components of current PD offerings include: a two-week long summer Tech Academy, availability of Tech Coach support by content area during one period a day plus availability before and after school, Tech Tuesdays (one Tuesday a month the first 30 minutes of teacher plan time is dedicated to individual PD goal support, a Tech PD agenda item is presented during each monthly Early Release time, and the January in-service day is dedicated to Technology PD.

Board president, Ms. Jones, recognized that, in earlier days, some teachers were fearful, possibly because of technology "exposing what they didn't know." But she added, "Everyone can learn and the digital natives come in knowing how to manage."

Dr. Jutting summed it up with, "There is no professional development silver bullet. We don't have the answer although we've tried different approaches. We will continue to look for the best way to support our staff."

From where you sit, what is the greatest challenge for students making the shift to customized learning? How can you best support students in that journey?

Every parent, including board members, strongly agreed on two key points regarding 24/7 technology access. First and foremost, they appreciated the opportunities their children had with technology access and, specifically, that it was available during high school in advance of their entering a post-secondary setting. They clearly identified the "safety net" the school support provided for both parents and students as worthy of others' consideration. Those who had a WHS graduate valued that their child learned some tough life lessons on how to use technology responsibly before leaving high school. According to parents, the home and school partnership is vital. For example, the district shuts off Internet access from midnight until 5:00 a.m. This allows the district to complete necessary software updates, it supports students who struggle with setting limits, and it backs parents who may need assistance with technology oversight. Second, parents recognized that the personality and age of the student played a significant factor in the level of home and/or school support or intervention needed. They encourage other parents to understand that there is "no one size fits all." As a result, one child might never have an issue with their laptop while another will need a parent to set limits including a "shut down or re-boot" time when the laptop is off limits.

Dr. Jutting observed, This level of access can lead to undisciplined behavior. They have to adjust to the laptop as a 'tool-for-use' versus 'an entertainment center.' Administrators, board members, and parents valued that students were learning these lessons in high school rather than at the post-secondary level where the stakes are higher. Each gave examples of working together to scaffold students' learning to become savvy consumers of technology and self-directed learners.

Both administrators commented, "The middle 50% of students recognize all our efforts on behalf of students in danger of not graduating. They understand it's important. But they also feel like they are missing out and they are not getting the same level of attention." Dr. Butts identified "increased online courses for the middle group" as a viable way to address their concern and both administrators view the Middle College concept, which is under discussion, as another strategic avenue to address student interests.

Once students make the shift to customized learning, the rewards are sweet. Each interviewee proudly pointed out that post-secondary institutions and employers recognize WHS graduates' technology skill set. Dr. Jutting noted, "In the local workforce they are hired to help with networking. While in college they often are paired with other students as mentors. If they become educators, they naturally integrate technology to customize their teaching and student's learning."

Please share a "snapshot" that you believe best captures the positive impact of technology access on customized teaching and learning.

School Board Member Snapshot:

From her nine years as a laptop parent and seven years as a board member, Ms. Jones observed, "You have to fight for progressiveness in education. This was all very controversial when we started. People thought we were crazy at the time; you should have seen the headlines! But it was worth it." It goes without saying that she was beaming with pride when she added, "Today, recruiters and colleges recognize a Watertown kid!"

High School Principal Snapshot:

Dr. Butts reflected on breaking the mold with an alternative education student who had both academic and behavior challenges. George (not his real name) "couldn't get both oars in the water at the same time. He was 16 or 17 and still hadn't earned Algebra 1 credit but once he got connected with the right teacher, he finished in mid-October. Originally, he was just in credit recovery but we shifted gears to credit acceleration and he moved on to successfully earn both Geometry and Algebra II credit in one year. George finished his junior year and almost had his senior year completed when he moved to Spearfish where he completed his credits and graduated. Although he didn't get to complete at WHS, I believe if we hadn't customized for him at the point we did, he would not have graduated from Spearfish. George is a WHS success story and an example of our efforts to graduate 100% of our students." Sitting just a bit taller and with his chest out just a bit further, Dr. Butts ended with, "We *are* customizing teaching and learning."

Superintendent Snapshot:

"Ten years ago, when we went to the school board to request $500,000 to fund the 1:1 initiative, there was a strong voice that was 'anti-' the adoption. Many parents and community members questioned the wisdom of the investment. The tipping point in the discussion occurred when a student came forward to the podium. "Thank you for giving me the same opportunity as other kids. My family can't afford a computer." According to Dr. Juttting, that ended the budget conversation. "I'll never forget that moment. It's when the board decided to level the playing field."

◎ "Show Me the Data!"

In 1996 Tom Cruise played a movie character named Jerry Maguire, who frequently demanded, "Show me the money." Putting a spin on the phrase, you may be thinking, "Show me the data!"

The board president specifically identified the data challenge in these terms, "Although the district is very data-driven, it is hard to prove that technology access will raise test scores or ACT's. Some board members want to see data that show test scores have improved, which is hard to prove, but it will create well-rounded 21st Century Skills. It will produce well rounded learners." She also shared that while perception survey data were available, some individuals discounted the results because the data are based on "feelings or self-reporting."

While acknowledging the challenges identified by Ms. Jones, administrators highlighted positive WHS trend data, which validate efforts directed at achieving the 100% graduation rate goal supported by technology tools. Those tools have provided the opportunity for customization of teaching and learning.

- Over the past five years, WHS's ACT scores have been at or above the statewide ACT average. South Dakota ACT scores are above the national ACT average.
- The number of students who are off-grade level entering tenth grade, has decreased by 77%. In 2006-2007, 60 freshmen were off grade level. The average for the past three years is 14 students off grade-level. According to Dr. Butts, "Programs such as Credit Recovery, Transition Room, Graduation Coaches, and the ICU philosophy have contributed to the reduction of off grade level students."
- Course failure rate for grades nine through twelve has dropped from 15% in 2007-2008 to 8.5% in 2010-2011. Dr. Butts credits the ICU philosophy as a driving factor in reducing failure at all grade levels.

- Credit recovery programs have reduced the dropout rate and increased the graduation rate. In 2007-2008, 46.5 credits were recovered as compared to 220 recovery credits in 2009-2010. The following year, the number of credits recovered dropped to 173.5. Dr. Butts predicts the downward trend will continue over time. "I anticipate that we will put ourselves out of business," referring to a decreased need for credit recovery as customized teaching and learning increases.
- The No Child Left Behind (NCLB) South Dakota Department of Education definition of graduation rate requires a graduate to successfully complete required course work within a four-year window. But what if WHS reviewed their data using a "four+ year" graduation window that stretches to five years? Using that lens, they have dramatically reduced their dropout rate. Using the extended graduation window, the dropout rate is reduced from 6.5% (72 students) in 2005-2006 to 2.2% (26 students) in 2010-2011.

○ Going Forward

What did I learn from my immersion in the Watertown story? A better question might be: What did I relearn?

- It all starts with the vision.
- The alignment of mission, identity, beliefs, capabilities, skills, and environment is key.
- Being passionate, brave, relentless and solution-based when pursuing the vision and mission moves us from "dreaming big" to "acting big."
- The technology is just a tool but coupled with the statements above, it allows us to customize teaching and learning as we prepare our students for the "Age of Empowerment" to which Chuck and Bea refer in *inevitable*.
- Stakeholder support and authentic engagement is essential; even as it needs to be sustained, it is sustaining.

Courageous leadership is in evidence at all levels, and each leader focuses on creating conditions for the next level's success. Ultimately, students reap the benefit. What is my final thought?

This is no "old school"; this is truly a "**BOLD** school!"

1399334R00091

Made in the USA
San Bernardino, CA
14 December 2012